HIGHWAYS TO THE HIGHLANDS

FROM OLD WAYS TO NEW WAYS

ERIC SIMPSON

AMBERLEY

I dedicate this book to my daughter Rhona, my son Moray, my partner Anne and to Dawn, the widow of my deceased son Fraser.

First published 2021

Amberley Publishing
The Hill, Stroud,
Gloucestershire, GL5 4EP

www.amberley-books.com

ISBN: 978 1 4456 9924 0 (print)
ISBN: 978 1 4456 9925 7 (ebook)

British Library Cataloguing in Publication Data.
A catalogue record for this book is available from the British Library.

Typeset in 10pt on 13pt Celeste.
Origination by Amberley Publishing.
Printed in the UK.

Contents

Introduction

Whether for work or leisure we are accustomed to travelling long distances, taking our roads for granted unless we meet with some unwonted hindrance or delay. But how often do we think about the history of the highways that we travel on? All our roads, and bridges too, have a story of some kind or other. For centuries tourists and other travellers have been travelling and this book explores the history and heritage of the principal highways to and from the Highlands of Scotland. We trace the main roads north, showing, using contemporary and vintage illustrations, how they and the towns and villages en route have changed over time. We start, as many have over the years, by following the Great North Road from Edinburgh to Inverness. Our route then continues up the east coast to John o'Groats, before going round the north of Scotland from east to west. Here we link up with the current highly popular North Coast 500 tourist route and continue with it down the stunning west coast before returning to Inverness. Unlike the North Coast 500 route, we don't finish at Inverness, but stay on the west coast except when we go inland to Glenshiel returning to the west via the Great Glen and the Caledonian Canal. The next part'/south is equally spectacular, going by Fort William, Glencoe, and Loch Lomond to Glasgow, now a tourist hotspot in its own right. There are, of course, alternative roads to the north, but from these two main routes offshoot roads can be explored, leading to historic beauty spots like the Trossachs, Skye and the other magical islands of the west and north.

Many different travellers have used these highways, including early tourists like poets Robert Burns and William Wordsworth. While the well-to-do rode on horseback or in a carriage, the great majority walked, some for pleasure but most because there was no alternative. Up until the mid-nineteenth century, great droves of cattle and sheep en route to southern markets might also have been seen on what were originally mere tracks. Indeed, as we illustrate, the first made roads in the Highlands were military ones built to help suppress Highland rebels. Later road and bridge builders like Thomas Telford often followed the same basic routes. These engineers provided the foundation for a transport revolution. By the early nineteenth century many of these roads were turnpike roads paid for by tolls levied on the road users, which brings us to the comparatively short-lived stagecoach era. Short-lived it may have been, but it was a transforming era.

The artist John Charles Maggs manages to convey the thrill and excitement of a fast-moving stagecoach, in this instance the Great Yarmouth Mail. (Public domain)

Until 1823 Auld Cramond Brig was an essential link in the north road. It was closed to vehicular traffic in 1986. (Author's collection)

The development of the stagecoach network made a dramatic impact on the society of that time. The crack stagecoaches were the glamour vehicles and their drivers the knights of the road. Indeed the young bucks of the day vied for the honour of taking a spell at the reins.

Some of the physical evidence of that time can still be traced – toll houses and change inns (where coach horses were changed) for example. Surviving coaching inns enjoyed a renaissance when the roads, at the end of the nineteenth century, became busy again. Cycling had by now become incredibly popular, and as well as numerous cyclists on the roads, there was a gradually increasing number of motorists. The Highland roads, nevertheless, remained little changed until, in the interwar years, a major programme of road building and reconstruction was undertaken. As happened with the earlier phases of road development, the engineers of the 1920s and 1930s, and those who followed them, built on, and as often as not, over, the work of their predecessors. As illustrated here, traces of our old road systems can still be seen, even along our main highways.

Ever-increasing traffic in more recent times has seen the building of even more impressive structures like the two road bridges across the Firth of Forth and in the Highlands new bridges for the Beauly, Cromarty and Dornoch Firths, and also at Ballachulish and Kylesku. Road improvement continues to this day with the parts of the Great North Road from Edinburgh to Inverness not already dual carriageway now being duelled.

...and yet, this New Road will some day be the Old Road too, with ghosts on it and memories.

Neil Munro The New Road (1914)

1

Edinburgh to Dunkeld

Leaving the city for the north and north-east of Scotland we follow a route that, with some alterations, has long historic roots. This is the north road from Edinburgh to Dundee and Aberdeen and also, directly and indirectly, to a large part of the Highlands. This road was important for commercial, social, industrial and, for long periods of time, military reasons. The vital highway from Edinburgh to the north was Scotland's Great North Road. The historic Great North Road went from Edinburgh to South Queensferry, then crossing the Firth of Forth by ferry and continuing north to Perth. Today, if we are motorists, we go in the same direction, but the road is now termed the A90, becoming the M90 to cross the Firth by the new Queensferry Crossing and continuing in that guise until it reaches the Perth bypass where it joins the A9 coming from the central lowlands. The A9 takes us on to Inverness and then on to the far north. Pedestrians, cyclists and travellers by bus, however, still cross the Firth by the old road bridge completed in 1964.

Obviously the highway of today has undergone many changes in the course of time, involving, for example, removing obstructions and eliminating hazards by building bridges over narrow valleys and gorges. In Edinburgh the construction of Thomas Telford's 106-feet-high Dean Bridge over the Water of Leith in 1831 was a major development. It is a testimony to Telford's design that the Dean Bridge is still in use and today carries a far heavier weight of traffic than anyone could possibly have envisaged at the time it was built. At the city's eastern outskirts the construction of a new bridge across the River Almond was part of a scheme of road realignment carried out in the 1820s under the supervision of another distinguished Scottish engineer, John Rennie. In 1963 this fine eight-arch bridge was blown up using charges of gelignite to make way for the present concrete one. Fortunately, the much older crossing, the Old Cramond Brig, continues in use but for cyclists and pedestrians only.

The construction of Rennie's Cramond Bridge was part of the road improvements that were being implemented over large parts of Scotland in the second half of the eighteenth century and the first half of the nineteenth century. Major road works, of course, never come cheap and governments in normal circumstances are loath to dole out cash for them. In this period of laissez-faire government cash was not forthcoming, except, as we shall see, in the special case of the Highlands. Most significant highway improvements were carried out by trusts which had come into being because of the inadequacies of the former system. Previously, under the 1669 Statute Labour Act, any necessary work was carried out by local labour. This act demanded that the male inhabitants of the various parishes were required to work on their local roads for up to six days a year. It was a system that was unpopular with these usually reluctant 'conscripts'. As they were generally unskilled, it was also inefficient. A new system was gradually put into effect whereby Parliament allowed the influential men of an area to create turnpike trusts that then took responsibility for a stretch of road. These trusts were then responsible for supervising the construction and necessary repairs of their particular road. To pay for this work, the trusts were entitled to charge road users, and to this end toll houses with gates or bars, otherwise known as turnpikes, were therefore needed. The term turnpike also came to apply to a road that was tolled.

Planning for the Edinburgh to Queensferry Road commenced in 1751 with the passing by Parliament of the Midlothian Turnpike Trusts Act. A central board for the whole county was created, but most of the management for the road north from Edinburgh to Queensferry was delegated to the Cramond District Trust. The outcome was a turnpike road reckoned to be 'one of the most splendid in Scotland'. Each turnpike trust had its list of regulations. The Cramond Trust, for instance, prohibited bonfires, also setting off squibs

The still-occupied toll house at Cramond was only one of several hundred in south-east Scotland, but not too many still survive. (Author, 2019)

An eighteenth-century image of Gairneybridge tollhouse and turnpike gate on the old north road, south of Kinross. (Courtesy of Professor David Munro)

and other fireworks 'within 80 feet of the road'. Hawkers, gypsies and other travellers were forbidden to set up camp on the turnpike or on the verges. Sports like cricket, football, and tennis were also banned from the turnpike if they were a nuisance to passengers, likewise bull-baiting.

The installation of toll bars was met with many complaints and much grumbling about what seemed to be another form of taxation and 'an interference to trade'. While some people sought to avoid toll charges by seeking alternative routes, generally speaking toll charges were accepted, albeit reluctantly. Nevertheless, there were occasional outbreaks of violence with attacks on toll keepers and destruction of toll gates. Mobs destroyed a toll gate at Wick in 1827 and, as we shall see later, at Dunkeld in 1868. Toll houses could also suffer – one on the outskirts of Kirkcaldy was repeatedly pulled down by irate villagers.

Toll charges would have been accepted much less readily if there had been no great improvement in the condition of the roads. The early decades of the nineteenth century, however, saw great changes in methods of road construction. In these developments two figures stood out: Thomas Telford (1857–1834) and John MacAdam (1756–1836). Telford was an all-round engineer with a number of great works to his credit in England and Wales. In Scotland his most important road improvements were, as will be explained later, in the Highlands. Wherever they were built his roads were generally well engineered, but his construction methods were expensive. This is where John Louden MacAdam – another Scot – scored. He described and implemented a method of road construction that gave good results, but was markedly cheaper than Telford's. MacAdam's methods were so universally accepted that his name was applied to them, with roads built according to his system described as macadamised. Thus words like macadam and macadamisation entered the English language. When later generations added tar to the mix, the terms tar-macadam and tarmac were coined.

Stagecoaches were now able to travel much faster and road improvement was only one of several reasons for this. There had also been a step forward in coach design and, on the premium routes especially, the change-over times for passengers and horses alike had likewise been transformed. For an entertaining fictional account of the old and casual ways of operating a coach service we just need to read the opening pages of Sir Walter Scott's novel *The Antiquary*. The novelist gives a vivid account of a ramshackle public coach, known variously as the Queensferry *Diligence* or Hawes *Fly*, which plied between Edinburgh's High Street and South Queensferry, which was the departure point for the ferry across the Firth of Forth. Though the novel was published in 1816, Scott set his novel twenty-two years earlier in 1794 and, as he testified, 'there were many such [lackadaisical] services at that time'. For those who could afford it, an alternative was to travel 'post'. This meant either taking your own carriage or alternatively hiring a chaise or a gig. In both cases horses would be hired from change inns. Although coaches and their mode of operation had been greatly improved, Scott, in his later and more infirm years, preferred to post when travelling between his Abbotsford dwelling and Edinburgh. There is an informative entry in his journal (14 May 1827) that gives us comparative costs: 'To town per Blucher coach, well stowed and crushed, but saved cash, coming off for less than £2; posting costs nearly five, and you don't get on so fast by one-third.' It is important to emphasise that, until comparatively recent times, the great majority of those travelling on any road would have been riding or walking. Few, however, would have been walking for pleasure. That only began to be fashionable in the early 1800s.

The popular Kirklands Hotel was one of several stagecoach inns in Kinross, all competing for business. (Author, 2020)

John Frederick Herring's striking painting of a fully laden Edinburgh and London Royal Mail coach. (Multimedia Commons)

As the road north from North Queensferry to Perth was of national importance, the three counties involved – Fife, Kinross and Perth – shared the administration of the turnpike trust set up for it. The relevant Act of Parliament was passed in 1753, and with the very first toll house was erected three years later at Jamestown just outside Inverkeithing. The original route out of North Queensferry over the Ferry Hills proved to be too steep, so an easier route was selected, and this meant providing a new toll house. The replacement toll has long gone, but the name Ferrytoll survives at Inverkeithing with a well-used Bus Park and Ride helping to perpetuate the name.

As coach services improved, so demand increased. Around 1798 a Royal Mail coach service was introduced from Edinburgh to Aberdeen via Queensferry. Although provided in the main for speedy carrying of the Royal Mail, some passengers were also carried. The guards, unlike the coach drivers, were government employees and were armed with a blunderbuss and a pair of pistols. In the event of a blockage on the road or coach failure, the mail took priority. For those who could afford the extra expense, the 'Mail', as it was commonly called, was the stagecoach of choice. With industry and commerce growing in the first decades of the nineteenth the number of travellers using the roads also grew. Travelling for pleasure was also now in fashion, not with everyone but certainly with the moneyed classes. Many of society's upper class were eager to broaden their horizons and see more of the world. While the Grand Tour of Europe had long been regarded as an essential part of the education of the sons of the aristocracy, shorter tours within Britain had also become fashionable, thus increasing the pressure to improve the road system. The cult of romanticism in art and literature increased the number of visitors to Scotland. The new fashion was now to appreciate nature for its own sake, and Scotland, the Highlands in particular, had come into focus as a strange place of romance and dramatic beauty. In consequence, there were many more coaches, and other kinds of vehicles too, running on all the main highways. By 1838 the mail and stagecoach departures to Queensferry and beyond from Edinburgh included the *Caledonian* for Inverness via Perth three days a week. There were five daily coaches for Aberdeen, four via Cupar and Dundee and one by Perth. The reason why the route to the north-east via Cupar came to be preferred to the Great North Road was because Burntisland, which had with a superior ferry service, had outstripped Queensferry as the main ferry port for Fife.

The social impact of fast-moving stagecoaches was very considerable. Stagecoaches carried the latest news to the people in the towns along its route. Thomas de Quincy wrote an eyewitness account of how the Royal Mail coaches that left the General Post Office in London each evening for all parts of the kingdom celebrated the victories of the Napoleonic Wars (1803–1815). When a victory had been announced, the mail coaches departed one after the other, each one decorated – 'horses, men, carriages, all are dressed in laurels and flowers, oak leaves and ribbons.' Thus the glad news was conveyed from town to town to the furthest corners of the land. It was a mail coach that first brought to the news of the British naval victory at Trafalgar in 1805 Kinross. As at the same time the people of Kinross learned that Admiral Nelson had died at the moment of victory, it was for them an occasion for 'great grief and great joy'.

Perth's Salutation Hotel was a busy coaching inn. In 1745 Bonnie Prince Charlie was a temporary 'guest' there. (Author, 2019)

Although the toll house on Smeaton's 1771 bridge across the River Tay at Perth was used in that capacity for only five years, it is still there. (Author, 2019)

The gentry and members of the nobility now heading to Scotland in ever-increasing numbers also demanded better standards of accommodation and this was reflected in the number of new stagecoach inns erected in the first half of the nineteenth century. There are still some fine examples of the inns that were built around that time. Periodic breaks were essential for coach crews and passengers, but even more so for the horses that provided the means of propulsion. The crack coaches of the day like Captain Barclay's *Defiance* going to Aberdeen travelled at speeds of 10 to 12 miles per hour. Coaches moving at that speed, which was fast for those days, needed a change of horses every twelve miles or so. Changes were carried out only at the larger inns like South Queensferry's Hawes Inn – change inns they were called. From the standpoint of the postal authorities four minutes was deemed sufficient to change a team for the Mail. For the Royal Mail speed of change over, as with racing car pit stops, was all important.

Kinross was an important staging town with several change inns and that brought a measure of rivalry between the ostlers of the different inns. Traditionally Scottish inns had a poor reputation, especially in the more remote parts, but as demand for their services increased so did standards. In 1799, Robert Heron lavished praise on Kinross's 'two clean, convenient inns' and their civil and attentive landlords. The same author further remarked on the number of visitors coming this way en route to tour the Highlands. This, he added, was because a tour of the Highlands had become 'from various circumstances a fashionable summer tour'. The ancient burgh, now city, of Perth also had a long history as a staging post for travellers to the important cities of Dundee and Aberdeen and also for those going further north into the Highlands. Perth is notable for the number of surviving toll houses, even including one on Smeaton's elegant 1771 bridge over the Tay. In 1848 Queen Victoria, on one of her sojourns into the Highlands, broke her journey at Perth and it is a measure of the way that Scotland's inns had been transformed that she elected to stay at the George Inn, which of course was duly renamed the Royal George Hotel. A copy of the Royal Warrant is on display in the hotel foyer.

From Perth the traveller has a choice of routes, several of which would take you into the Highlands. They include the A93 to Braemar and the Deeside Highlands, but our preoccupation here is with the Great North Road which, joins the A9 west of Perth. Sixteen miles or so further on, we enter the Pass of Birnam, which is one of the historic entry points to the Highlands and, when the autumn colours are at their best, a magnificent one. Although the twin villages of Birnam and Dunkeld are bypassed by the A9 road, both are well visiting. At Dunkeld, the River Tay is crossed by a handsome bridge built in 1809 by Thomas Telford with the 4th Duke of Atholl bearing the brunt of the cost. When the bridge was built, the new North Road was aligned with it, and in consequence it became the main shopping street. Shops were built along this street to catch the passing traffic, likewise two major hotels – the Royal Dunkeld Hotel (c. 1820) and the Atholl Arms (1833). Meanwhile, the bridge tolls extracted by the 5th Duke became increasingly unpopular. In 1868 riots broke out and the toll gates were tossed into the river. However,

THE HOTEL, BRIDGE OF CALLY

For travellers going to Braemar and the Deeside Highlands, the Bridge of Cally Hotel was, and still is, a popular stop on the A93. (Author's collection)

The ornamental nature of the toll house on the south side of Telford's Dunkeld Bridge is a reflection of the Duke of Atholl's status. (Author, 2018)

The Atholl Arms Inn, as it was originally, enjoyed the benefit of its strategic location as the very first building to be encountered on crossing the bridge and entering Dunkeld. (Author, 2019)

Visitors to Dunkeld and Birnam were encouraged to visit the Hermitage, a spectacular Atholl Estate Folly, now in the care of the National Trust for Scotland. (Author, 2018)

it was another eleven years before the bridge tolls were removed. By that time virtually all tolls had disappeared, and the turnpike system was also abolished. When the local government system was reformed in 1889 responsibility for roads, but not those in towns, was transferred to county councils.

Birnam, on the southern side of Telford's Tay Bridge, is largely a Victorian settlement that owed its growth to the adjacent railway station built in 1856. For seven years the village was the railway's northern terminus, which meant that travellers proceeding further into the Highlands had to transfer to a coach at Birnam. This was obviously to the benefit of the Birnam Hotel, built around that time. Beatrix Potter, as a young girl, was a holiday resident in the area and is commemorated by a Beatrix Potter Garden. It was in Birnam that she wrote her first story, *The Tale of Peter Rabbit*.

2

Dunkeld to Dalwhinnie

The first 'made' road, as opposed to drove road, linking Dunkeld to Inverness was one of the military roads built in the wake of the 1715 Jacobite Rebellion to assert control of the government of the United Kingdom. These roads, built by redcoat troops under the command of General Wade, linked forts that were built to house the army of occupation. However, roads that served the needs of the Hanoverian army of occupation did not meet the needs of later generations. Nor did they extend much beyond the Great Glen and that was an area with, especially in the west, inadequate communications. It was thanks once more to government intervention in the early 1800s that we see the next great phase of road building in the Highlands. This was because the government in London was worried that the then current large-scale emigration of Highlanders would lead to a loss of a valuable reservoir of fighting men for the British armed forces. To keep the Highlanders at home, Parliament decided to provide employment for adult men by improving communications, a measure that would also help to alleviate poverty in the area. One result was the construction of the Caledonian Canal linking the east and west. A Parliamentary Commission had been set up to oversee this enterprise with the task of its implementation given to Thomas Telford. At the same time, the workaholic Telford, in addition to work he was engaged in south of the border, was also supervising another mammoth project, namely the construction in the Highlands of a large number of new roads, bridges and harbours. Once again a Parliamentary Commission, a separate one, had been appointed as the overseeing body. The arrangement was that the government paid for half of any roads constructed, and the landowners had to meet the rest. As a result, between 1803 and 1821, when the work of construction was completed, a remarkable 920 miles of road and over 1,100 bridges had been built – a truly remarkable achievement.

On the Great North Road, Telford and his engineers followed Wade's route through the Central Highlands to Inverness, albeit with some significant alterations. Over the 115 miles – as then measured – from Perth to Inverness, much of the work really involved repairing and reconstructing existing roads. The government continued to meet the whole expense of maintenance of the military roads until 1814, when responsibility for their upkeep was transferred to the county landowners. The Perthshire lairds, however, led by the Duke of Atholl, initially refused to pay their share. Only in 1823, with the county

The north road had to bear all sorts of loads. This one was destined for a hydro-electric power station. (Courtesy of Alan Brotchie)

Some of Pitlochry's plentiful supply of hotels and restaurants feature in this photograph dating to *c.* 1930. This is Atholl Road, formerly part of the Atholl Turnpike. (Author's collection.)

highways on the verge of becoming impassable, did they concede defeat. The work of reconstruction was commenced under the supervision of Telford's right-hand man in Scotland, John Mitchell, who, on his death in 1824, was succeeded as Principal Inspector by his young son, Joseph. To pay for work on the Atholl Turnpike section of the Great North Road tolls were levied, with the first toll houses erected in 1823. From Edinburgh to Inverness and beyond, the turnpike system was seen as the best way to ensure that the main highways at least were kept in good order, which was more than could be said for the Atholl Estate Office. In 1827 the Atholl turnpike toll cash, which had been stored in the estate office, was stolen by an office employee. To the great anger of the Duke neither the thief nor his loot were ever traced.

Prior to the building of the present A9 road, the main north road went through a number of small settlements which benefited in consequence. Ballinluig, on the east side of the River Tay and 4 miles or so south of Pitlochry, is an exception, as it is owes its origin to the railway. It had a station that was a junction because the branch line to Aberfeldy left the main Highland line there. Ironically, with both station and branch line closed, Ballinluig now survives by providing services for motorists and truckers. Pitlochry, although it benefited greatly from highway improvements, owed its initial growth to being on Wade's road. General Wade had opted for this lower route, as did the builders of the Atholl Turnpike, in preference to the previous road via Moulin, which up until then had been the focal point of the parish. Moulin, with its inn and kirk, was left to slumber quietly on. By 1839 Pitlochry, on the other hand, was growing with new shops, banks and a new inn – the progenitor of what is now Fisher's Hotel. The Pitlochry we see today is, like Birnam, largely a Victorian creation, owing much of its growth, firstly, to the re-routing of the main road and, secondly, to its growing popularity as a fashionable holiday centre. This popularity was boosted by recommendations from Queen Victoria's physician and the arrival of the railway in 1865. Industrialists from Glasgow and other industrial towns built holiday homes in Pitlochry so that they and their families could escape the smoke and grime of the cities where they made their fortunes. Men who had run the empire as merchants and administrators likewise saw the town's its fresh, clean air as a suitable retirement abode.

Killiecrankie a few miles away was where the dashing Viscount Dundee, fighting for the exiled King James VII and II, fell in the moment of victory. The pro-Jacobite Highland clansmen had won a famous victory but, without their charismatic leader, their advance was halted at Dunkeld after another ferocious battle. The gorge formed by the River Garry has long attracted tourists. For the author of Rhind's *Scottish Tourist* (*c.* 1847) it was a wild and savage place: 'the tourist will now enter the celebrated and sublime Pass of Killiecrankie with a feeling that approaches to terror.' By the end of the century tourists had evidently become more blasé, as Murray's 1892 *Handbook* just saw it as 'one of the most charming walks in Highland Scotland'.

In the 1920s the Great North Road north of Perth, little changed since Telford's time, was the subject of many complaints. From Dalnacardoch to Dalwhinnie the road was little more than a mountain track. The increasing use of motor vehicles brought demands for road widening and better road surfaces, this last now possible with the use of tar-macadam. In consequence, in 1924 the Ministry of Transport, a wartime creation, offered generous grants to local authorities for the construction of roads of national importance, trunk

Above: The Allt Essan toll house near Killiecrankie was built for the Atholl Turnpike Trustees in 1823 at a cost of £80. (Author, 2018)

Left: 'Ye'll tak the high road and I'll take the low road.' What the up-aloft road users don't see. Completed in 1986, the Killiecrankie viaduct was the last section of the 'new' A9 to be built. (Author, 2017)

roads they were later called. Roads were also being classified and the Great North Road, now recognised as a trunk road, became the A9 with its northern terminus at Inverness. In 1935 that was altered to John o'Groats, then in 1997 changed again but this time to Scrabster. Only a road bridge to Orkney could lead to a further extension to the A9. The start of the A9, originally in Edinburgh, now begins at the pleasingly named Cadger's Brae Roundabout just outside Grangemouth. The A9 of today was built in the seventies and eighties, but many sections of the previous highways survive and, including some paths, form the National Cycling route NCN7.

The village of Blair Atholl came into being when the Thomas Telford-era north road was rerouted. Sections of the older highway – part built by Wade, part estate-built – can still be followed. Notable landmarks on the old highway include the Auld Brig of Tilt and Old Blair, the latter where the walkers car park is situated. The walk up Glen Tilt from there is to be recommended and enthusiastic hikers can follow the old drove road right through to Deeside. Pedestrians were not always welcome, however. In 1847 the Duke of Atholl and his minions made an unsuccessful attempt to block the way for a party from Edinburgh University who had come all the way from Braemar. This was a cause celebre at the time and it led to legal proceedings which was were won by the recently founded Scottish Rights of Way Society. During the 1745 Jacobite Rising, as in the 1715 rising, the Murray family of Atholl was divided. Lord George Murray, the sixth son of the 1st Duke and one of Prince Charles' leading generals, had the unusual experience of besieging his family home, Blair Castle. The 2nd Duke, who had remained loyal to George II, had the towers and battlements

The transformer shown on page 18 was bound for the Grampian hydro-electric power station at Tummel Bridge, which dates back to 1933. It is now part of a much larger scheme. (Author's collection)

This smartly dressed couple with an early twentieth-century motorbike and sidecar with a Dundee registration have no parking problems on this quiet Highland road. (Courtesy of Alan Brotchie)

removed, which made it, critics said, look more like a factory than a castle. When the Scots baronial style came into vogue, the 7th Duke restored the castellated features. Two miles on from Blair Atholl, we arrive at Bruar, the site of a toll house in coaching days. The Clan Donnaicdh Centre has taken its place. There was an inn here too, the Bruar Falls Inn, but that has been replaced by a sizeable retail enterprise – the House of Bruar, now a destination in its own right. However, the spectacular Falls of Bruar have ensured that Bruar has been on the tourist map for a very long time. That the area round the Falls is well wooded is thanks to Robert Burns, who wrote some verses to the landowner, the Duke of Atholl, extolling the 'wild roaring' falls, but also expressing the need for trees and shrubs to ornament the surrounds.

From Bruar onwards, the landscape is barer, and there are no villages until Dalwhinnie is reached. Instead we pass many signs to shooting lodges. The first, Dalnacardoch by the River Tummel, is where the military road from Stirling via Crieff joined the north road. General Wade spent some time there in 1729, staying in a hut while supervising work on what he called his Great Highland Road. Bishop Forbes recorded stopping for a meal at Dalnacardoch Inn on his journey north in 1762 and again on his return later that year. When the stagecoaches stopped running, the inn became redundant too and was turned into a shooting lodge. With most of the traffic going on the trains, the roads became badly

Dalnacardoch on the road north was also the turn-off for the former military road to Stirling. A short distance along this road brings us to Garry Bridge, and Bridge a fine example of a Wade-era bridge. (Author, 2017)

The Ebendon toll house features in this postcard of the newly resurfaced (*c.* 1928) north road a short distance to the north of Dalnacardoch. (Author's collection)

neglected. The next shooting lodge Dalnaspidal, as its name suggests, had been in the distant past a 'spittal' or hospice for travellers. The 'dal' place element, common hereabouts, derives from dail, meaning a riverside meadow. In the more recent past, there was a railway station here. While there weren't many people around, there were lots of animals with 17,845 sheep shipped from Dalnaspidal in 1890. With most traffic going to the trains, the roads were allowed to deteriorate. In the *Contour Road Book of Scotland* (first edition 1898), we read that the road was satisfactory as far as the Struan Inn (on the opposite side of the A9 from House of Bruar), but then the surface worsened until 'in some parts it is little else than a loose mass of stones, in others overgrown with grass'. Cyclists, in fact, were advised to take the train for the next 20 miles from Struan to Dalwhinnie.

The Pass of Drumochter, 1,508 feet/460 metres at the highest point, was one of the main routes for cattle droves coming from the Western and Northern Highlands. On his journey south in 1762 Bishop Forbes overtook no fewer than eight droves of cattle, comprising 1,200 animals in all, spread over a mile and heading for Crieff Tryst (market). The cattle, he ascertained, had come from Skye and were owned by Macdonald of Flodigarry. Further on, where the road passes close to Loch Garry, the Bishop saw yet another drove – 300 or so, also bound for Crieff. In later years Falkirk was more favoured as the trysting place for cattle coming from the Highlands. Cattle on the hoof to Falkirk are no more, but what is very evident are massive electricity pylons marching over the hills carrying power to the south not quite to Falkirk but to an electrical sub-station at nearby Denny.

Well situated on the great North Road, the Grampian Tea Rooms and Filling Station at Dalwhinnie did good business selling teas and petrol. (Author's collection)

This young couple in their dashing Morgan three-wheeler, off on a camping holiday, have halted where the signpost points to Badenoch. (Author's collection)

The cattle Bishop Forbes encountered would have rested overnight at one of the many 'stances' on the road south. As cattle could not be rushed and sufficient time for grazing had to be allowed, a drove would cover only 10 to 12 miles a day. In droving days Dalwhinnie was, like Dalnacardoch and Dalnaspidal, an overnight stance for cattle, its river meadows providing both nourishment and water. Two drove roads met there – one from the Inverness direction, the other from the west via the Corrieyairack Pass. As General Wade had selected the Corrieyairack for his link road to Fort Augustus, it meant that Dalwhinnie, the highest village in the Highlands, was also a junction for these major military roads. Ironically, the Corrieyairack was used by Prince Charles Edward Stuart for a speedy march south, enabling him to capture Edinburgh leaving and his opponent General Cope stranded in Inverness. By this point, travellers are well inside the Cairngorm National Park, which is twice the size of the Lake District and easily Britain's largest.

In October 1861 Queen Victoria and Albert, travelling incognito, paid a surprise visit to what was then the Dalwhinnie Inn. She wrote in *Our Life in the Highlands*: 'unfortunately there was hardly anything to eat, and there was only tea, and two miserable starved Highland chickens, without any potatoes! No pudding and no fun…' Their servants fared even worse, getting only the remnants of the two starved chickens. This was the second to last of their 'Great Expeditions'. Two months later Albert was dead.

3

Dalwhinnie to Dingwall

From Dalwhinnie the roads, both old and new, follow the course of the River Truim, a tributary of the Spey, which leads us to the Badenoch village of Newtonmore. Though Newtonmore and the other villages that bordered the River Spey were on the turnpike road, it was the arrival of the railway in 1863 that transformed their fortunes. The railway brought holidaymakers who valued clean, fresh air and who were keen on outdoor sports. Anglers had that great salmon river, the Spey, virtually on the doorstep. Houses were made available to rent and hotels built to cater for both long-stay and passing tourists, thus bringing a new prosperity to Badenoch and Strathspey. Unlike Newtonmore, its near neighbour Kingussie was planned, it having been the 4th Duke of Gordon's intention to create a prosperous industrial village. However, when Queen Victoria and Albert arrived in Kingussie while on the same journey that took them to Dalwhinnie, they found, 'a very straggling place with very few cottages' and little sign of the hoped-for industries. Kingussie, nevertheless, did prosper in time as, like its neighbours, it became a health resort.

At Aviemore we are now in Strathspey, and like so many of the settlements hereabouts largely depends on catering for tourists. Aviemore saw its first 'tourist development' with the building of a simple inn on General Wade's Great Road. Aviemore's real growth and development, however, came with the arrival of the Inverness & Perth Junction Railway in 1863 (from 1865 known as the Highland Railway). In early August the railway stations here and all over the Highlands were especially busy as the grouse shooting season started on 12 August – 'the Glorious Twelfth'. Aviemore still benefits from being on the main Inverness line. In addition, sections of old railway line have been brought back into use for a very popular heritage steam railway. By the 1930s and 1940s the pattern of holidays had changed. Middle class visitors were now touring by car and motor coach, often spending only one or two nights in one place. The advent of the motor-car brought changes that were not welcomed by all. Charles Plumb, writing in 1935, described Aviemore as a wretched place: 'The village consists of a mere line of petrol-pumps and tin shops planted at the side of the Great North Road...' One wonders what this purist would have thought of today's Aviemore, which has become a mini metropolis of the outdoor world with supermarkets and a plethora of outdoor sports shops and a suburban sprawl that has extended into the nearby woodlands. Plumb would no doubt have also criticised the access road built in 1961 for the Cairngorm

Pony Trekkers leaving their Headquarters

In the 1950s, with the days of the long-stay holiday over, the owners of Newtonmore's Balavil Hotel diversified into pony trekking. (Author's collection)

HIGH STREET, KINGUSSIE.

There is much more traffic in today's Kingussie, but compared with this *c.* 1930 Raphael Tuck image the high street is little changed. (Author's collection.)

Skiing developments. Elitist mountaineers of Plumb's era disapproved of roads and bridges that made access to the hills too easy. Completed in 1961, the ski road climbed to the Coire Cas chairlifts 2,000 feet up the mountain, bringing the Cairngorm massif closer both for skier and mountaineer. It is a great advantage, nonetheless, for Aviemore to be so close to the core of the Cairngorm National Park, namely Cairngorm mountain and its immediate neighbours. This is what some of the older generation consider the real Cairngorms.

Carrbridge, 10 miles north of Aviemore, is a classic example of a village that developed close to a crossing place – in this case a bridge, or rather a succession of bridges over the River Dulnain, a tributary of the Spey. The oldest is what remains of a 'coffin' bridge, which was badly damaged in the Muckle Spate of 1829. It had been built in 1717 to allow easier access to a nearby kirk and kirkyard. Since Wade's road to Inverness took a different line from today's road, his bridge over the Dulnain was a couple of miles west of the present village. That bridge was destroyed by flood. Its replacement (still extant) can probably be attributed to Major Caulfeild. The next bridge in the village would have been in the Telford era but it was replaced by the present concrete structure as part of the interwar road reconstruction schemes. As Carrbridge hosted a toll bar and the hostelry was a change inn, the village would have been a scene of bustling activity whenever a stagecoach arrived. The arrival of the railway to Aviemore in 1863 and subsequent extension to Carrbridge meant the end for that toll bar, no one wanting to take on an unprofitable let. On the other hand, the railway brought more visitors and the consequent enlargement of the hotel.

A Valentine postcard of the Aviemore Station Hotel in 1902. A year later another hotel, the Cairngorm, was built in front of it. (Author's collection)

Opened in 1966, the Aviemore Centre was an integrated holiday and recreation centre attracting young skiers like these to the Cairngorms. Much of it has now been demolished. (Author's collection)

A fine Caulfeild-era military bridge over the River Dulnain near Carrbridge. Its predecessor was destroyed by flood. (Author, 2019)

In the heart of Carrbridge we find the remnant of a 'coffin' bridge, built in 1717 and employed here as a platform to entertain the tourists. (Author, 2018)

If continuing to Inverness by the A9, the climb to the top of the Pass of Slochd Mor (1,328 feet / 405 metres), like the Drumochter Pass, could pose problems in the early days of motoring. We stay on the old road, however, which brings us to the striking Findhorn Bridge built c. 1928 near Tomatin. Close by, the Victorian-era railway viaduct is another notable piece of engineering. Before the Victorian era, there was a drovers' stance at Tomatin and in coaching days a toll bar and a change inn that was succeeded by a hotel, the Freeburn. After the hotel was demolished the site was occupied from 1986 to 2004 by a Little Chef restaurant, thus maintaining continuity of site use over a long period of time. This small village is probably best known today for the Tomatin Distillery, the largest malt whisky distillery in the world.

As for Inverness, although it was the capital of the Highlands its communications by road to the south were lamentable. Even after a coach service to Perth was introduced in 1800, four days were needed for the journey, with overnight stops at Carrbridge, Dalwhinnie and Blair Atholl. Since its timetables bore the adjunct 'If God permits', the coach was nicknamed 'the God permit'. In the event God did not permit and the business failed, but a few years later a more successful company was established. Telford's road improvements, including bridges like that at Dunkeld, increased the speed of travel and

On the way to Inverness, former robbers' den, the Pass of Slochd Mor (1328 feet /405 metres) posed a tough challenge to road and rail engineers alike. (Author's collection.)

The Findhorn Bridge over the river of the same name at Tomatin was one of four new concrete bridges built between 1925 and 1928 for the A9. (Author's collection)

ensured that travel by night, hitherto avoided, was now safe. By 1836 coaches could leave Edinburgh at 4 p.m. and arrive at Inverness next morning at around 10.30 a.m. By then too the townsfolk could boast of inns that 'for elegance and comfort are nowhere surpassed in Scotland'. When the railway came to Inverness with the completion of the Inverness & Nairn Railway in 1855, the enthusiasm with which it was greeted was a warning to the stagecoach proprietors and toll house keepers. The decline in value of toll bar lets was one sign of impending change as many were no longer profitable. By 1865, as at Carrbridge, fewer in the immediate area were being let, one of the exceptions being the Strathpeffer Bar. In this case, it was because the railway didn't reach this spa town until 1885.

In later years there was some nostalgia for the old days of four-in-hand coaches, since controlling a team of four required much more skill than the usual pair or single horse. In 1882 Andrew Carnegie took a party of friends in a four-in-hand coach all the way from Brighton to Inverness. In the 1890s Macrae & Dick Ltd advertised 'Old Times' four-in-hand coach excursions to local beauty spots, starting from Inverness railway station though. It is possibly no coincidence that it was in 1885 that Isabel Harriet G. Anderson published her book *Inverness before Railways*, which includes a full account of the different coaches

The restored Muirtown toll house by the canal basin, like the rest of Inverness's toll houses, was sited on the edge of town to catch incoming traffic. (Author, 2018)

ROYAL STUART MOTOR HOTEL

The Royal Stuart Motor Hotel was a motor age equivalent of a coaching inn. Both this name and its current, Drumossie Hotel, make a nod in the direction of the Culloden battlefield. (Author's collection)

and the service they provided. She could look back to a time when, for the greater part of the year, there were no fewer than eight stagecoaches leaving Inverness each day – coaches with names like *Star, Defiance, Duke of Wellington, Marquis of Breadalbane*, and *Caberfeidh,* as well as the mail coaches, one south to Edinburgh and one to the north. 'The *Defiance* Coach for Aberdeen,' the author recalled, 'started from Inverness every morning at six, and the inspiriting [sic] notes of its bugle woke many a dreamer from his slumbers at that hour. It was drawn by four grey horses, and formed a very enlivening sight, as it dashed into Inverness on the return journey at about half-past six in the evening.' She does add a note of realism by stating that coach interiors were anything but comfortable, particularly if closely packed. Judged by many other eyewitness accounts, that is probably an understatement.

Today the number of hotels and guesthouses in Inverness testify to continuing popularity with tourists. It was to the town's good fortune that, from 1933 onward, credulous observers have been seeing something unusual in Loch Ness, a creature that they claimed to be of monstrous size and shape. The newspapers battened on to the story, christening it the Loch Ness Monster, or Nessie in popular parlance, thus giving Inverness the kind of publicity that tourism promoters elsewhere can only dream of. For those who prefer a touch of realism, the National Trust Visitor Centre at Culloden battlefield, Urquhart Castle and Fort George, the barracks built for the victors at Culloden, are just a few of the sites that are worth visiting.

Herring drifters heading to the west coast from their east coast home ports via the Caledonian Canal. From 1864 Tomnahurich Hill in Inverness was used as a cemetery. (Author's collection)

A.4080.   DELMORE ROAD HOUSE, BEAULY ROAD, INVERNESS.

The 1930s Dalmore Road House and filling station, once owned by Highland Airways pioneer, Captain F. E. Fresson, is now an agency for motorcycles. (Author's collection)

Until well into the nineteenth century, for most tourists Inverness was as far north as they ever went. The northern counties of Scotland, the southern parts of Inverness-shire excepted, were virtually unknown territory. Sutherland and Caithness, in particular, received scant attention in the guidebooks. This was partly because of their distance from the main centres of population in the south and partly because of the poor communications and, with one notable exception, the consequent absence of public transport. The one exception was the mail coach that, beginning in 1819, connected Inverness to Thurso. As the *Scotsman* reported when it began, this completed 'the mail-coach conveyance from Falmouth to London and from London to the Northern Ocean' – a remarkable achievement for the time. It was only by having roads and bridges fit to bear a coach that this was now possible. Having inns at each stage to provide relief horses and suitable refreshment for coachmen and passengers was another essential feature. The road engineer John Mitchell described what travelling in the roadless areas of the Highlands used to mean: 'crossing dangerous rivers and streams, travelling in wet clothes, and for shelter living in smoky and wretched huts, where oatcakes, milk and whisky were the chief or only refreshments.'

For most of human history, three major estuaries were obstacles to travellers heading north by the east coast route. Plans for providing a direct and fast route north had been aired periodically, but it took the discovery of oil in Scottish waters and industrial developments in the Cromarty area to accelerate the process. The Cromarty Firth was the first to be bridged in 1979, the Kessock Bridge over the Beauly Firth came five years later and lastly in 1991 the Dornoch Bridge. Although the A9 leaves Inverness by the Kessock Bridge, for the purposes of this book we are, starting with the A862, taking the east coast road to Wick and Thurso, the same way as the old-time mail coaches. For us following in their wheel track, we leave Inverness by crossing the Caledonian Canal near to its eastern outlet (a walk out to the canal sea lock is recommended) and continue by the A862 on the south side of the Beauly Firth to Beauly. *Leigh's New Pocket Road-book of Scotland* (1836) gave the distance between Inverness and Wick as 137½ miles with the mail coach scheduled to stop at eighteen inns on the way. The first halt came at Bogroy Inn, now renamed the Old North Inn, followed by the Beauly Inn at 12¾ miles. To reach Beauly we have to cross the River Beauly by the Lovat Bridge (1814), one of the many bridges built by Thomas Telford. Beauly, which has after Beauley an interesting old priory and a good variety of shops, is still a popular break point for today's tourists.

Muir of Ord, a village that in cattle droving days was an important cattle market, comes next, and then Conon Bridge, the bridge there replacing the ferry at Scuddel. Telford's bridge over the River Conon has not survived, but the unusual two-storey octagonal toll house of 1828 has. It was designed by one of Telford's key assistants Joseph Mitchell. Mackenzie's Inn at Dingwall was the next scheduled stop for the mail coach. The town in those days, according to one guidebook, 'consists principally of one main street, from which several lanes converge,' and that is pretty well still true of Dingwall's town centre today. Dingwall is probably best known today as the home to a small football club with big ambitions – Ross County FC. The former spa town of Strathpeffer lies not far away and is still a popular holiday centre.

Left: Street names are useful clues to the past, as here with Ferry Road, Beauly. Not much remains to indicate that there had been an important ferry here over the River Beauly. (Anne Paterson 2020)

Below: Near to Dingwall, in the 1920s the former spa town of Strathpeffer was in the process of being transformed into a popular touring hub. (Author's collection)

The Square and Highland Hotel, Strathpeffer   3885

4

Dingwall to Helmsdale

The A862, which we have been following merges, with the A9 at the north end of the Cromarty Bridge. A more interesting route, however, is the road, the B817, along the north side of the Cromarty Firth via Evanton, Alness and Invergordon. After Invergordon join the A9 before diverting to Tain on the southern shore of the Dornoch Firth. All these Easter Ross communities have a story to tell and accomplish this with interesting display panels. The Black Rock gorge, an awesomely deep, narrow fissure near Evanton, features in *Harry Potter* with *and the Goblet of Fire*. Invergordon, thanks to its deep water harbour, has gained new importance, firstly as a base for the oil industry and more recently as a disembarkation point for coach tours & insert cruise ships. In coaching days it had an excellent inn, the Commercial, which in 1847 was the focal point in a riot. The inn was besieged by an angry mob of rioters trying to free some of their number who were held prisoner there. 1847 was a time of famine, particularly bad in Ireland and the West Highlands because of the failure of the potato crop. The fishing communities of the Moray Firth, having suffered a poor herring season, feared that they too would suffer famine and, accordingly, tried to stop the export of grain by blockading the local ports and harbours. To quell these disturbances, soldiers were despatched in a naval transport all the way from Portsmouth to Invergordon. In the early twentieth century, the Royal Navy returned, Invergordon being valued as an anchorage and supply base. In recent years oil rigs and cruise liners have, however, replaced warships. As well as a ferry across the Cromarty Firth to Balblair, there was one to Cromarty, a historic town well worth a diversion. The Nigg–Cromarty car ferry at the entrance to the Cromarty Firth (the narrowest point) is the last of the many ferries that once operated in the Eastern Highlands. Tain has a much older history, having been an ancient royal burgh and medieval place of pilgrimage. King James IV was a regular pilgrim to the shrine of St Duthac, one of Scotland's leading pilgrimage destinations. Latter-day pilgrims, however, may be heading instead to the local supermarkets or the James Braid-designed golf course. The town's spacious links and its golf course, plus a large number of listed buildings, make it well worth exploring on foot.

From Tain onward the A9, adhering closely to the line of the old coach road, takes us along the south shore of the Dornoch Firth to Ardgay and Bonar Bridge where there is a

The Foulis Storehouse near Evanton, one of the meal stores blockaded during the 1847 meal riots, now houses a restaurant, heritage centre and shop. (Anne Paterson, 2019)

From Invergordon there was a ferry across the Cromarty Firth to Balblair in the Black Isle. It cost six pence in 1898 (one shilling for a bicycle). There was also another to Cromarty. (Author's collection)

bridge across the Kyle of Sutherland. This was only one of a number of major bridges that Telford built in the north under the aegis of the High Commission for Roads and Bridges. Others included the Lovat Bridge across the River Beauly in 1814, the Conon Bridge in 1811 and the Helmsdale Bridge also in 1811 – thus dispensing with ferry crossings that were both inefficient and dangerous. The Meikle Ferry on the Dornoch Firth had a particularly bad reputation. In 1809 there was a dreadful accident when no fewer than ninety-nine passengers were drowned, and it was this tragedy that accelerated the construction of a bridge at Bonar. Telford's bridge of 1812 was destroyed by flood in 1892, and the present bridge is the third on this site. As the route by Bonar Bridge, as the village there came to be called, added extra miles to the journey north, the Meikle Ferry continued in use until 1957 but for passengers only latterly. There were other ferries of course in the Dornoch Firth area. This writer well remembers being rowed across the Kyle of Sutherland in a tiny rowing boat, bicycle perched precariously across the prow. This was a request service provided by an Invershin boatbuilder.

In coaching days, the Ross-shire Road Trustees together with their Sutherland equivalents were responsible for the upkeep for the bridge at Bonar. The trustees' minutes reveal that their expenses included the cost of repairing the damage caused by ships colliding with it. The Ross-shire Road Trustees certainly kept up to date by purchasing a stone crusher and a traction engine to haul it in 1874. The expenses included the purchase of red flannel to make flags, and payment for a man to walk in front of the traction engine waving one of the then mandatory red flags. When the Dornoch Firth was bridged in 1991, travellers no longer needed to go by Bonar Bridge, thus cutting 26 miles off their journey.

On Struil Hill, overlooking the Kyle of Sutherland, on the way to Carbisdale Castle Y.H.

Cyclists at the high point of the Struie Hill road admiring the view. The teenage Eric Simpson was similarly impressed when cycling this way. (Author's collection)

Stake net fishing for salmon near the replacement for Telford's bridge at Bonar, which was destroyed by flood. This one was replaced in 1973. (Author's collection)

Conveniently sited between Bonar Bridge and Dornoch, Macrae's Tearoom at Spinningdale (plus petrol pumps and shop) catered for the increasing number of visitors coming to the Highlands by car. (Author's collection)

Dornoch Cathedral dates back to the thirteenth century. It was gutted by fire in 1570 and restored in the 1830s at the behest of the Countess of Sutherland. Both she and the 1st Duke are buried here. (Author, 2019)

There is an alternative route to Bonar Bridge. Instead of taking the long way round by Tain, the B9176 over Struie Hill offers a shorter way. (see image on page 39)

Once across the Dornoch Firth we are in the historic County of Sutherland, in the early 1800s a county very much under the thumb of the Countess of Sutherland and her husband the Marquess of Stafford, who was created the Duke of Sutherland in 1833. The minutes of the Sutherland County Road Trust of that time reveal that the Marquess' agents – William Young, James Loch and Patrick Sellar – played an important role in the administration of the county's roads. It was Patrick Sellar who came up with a method of crossing the River Fleet and William Young who instigated the erection of toll bars on the North Road or, as they called it, 'the Great Post Road'. By 1817 five toll bars or gates were in operation with each toll keeper supplied with a good stone house. The toll house at Bonar Bridge was erected by Mr George Alexander, a Golspie house carpenter, at a cost of £94. Milestones being mandatory for turnpike roads, it was agreed that 'milestones of hard granite, properly hewn and numbered' be placed on the section of the North Road under their charge.

Although bypassed by the present-day A9, Dornoch, the county town for the old County of Sutherland, was on the mail couch route. From Tain onward, however, the mail couch was reduced to having just two horses instead of the usual four. Dornoch was not then famous for its golf links, and golf was a subject that did not even get a mention in Black's comprehensive 1851 *Guide*. Going north from Dornoch the Parliamentary road crossed Loch Fleet by a causeway-cum-bridge named, rather prosaically, the Mound. Thomas Telford's ingenious self-regulating gates on the bridge section at the north end of the

Mound allowed water from the River Fleet to flow out at low tide yet kept the incoming tides out. The ferry across Loch Fleet at the narrows near the mouth of the loch was called the Little Ferry. The tidal race here can be fierce. It greatly alarmed the young Donald Sage when he was on his way from his Kildonan home to school in Dornoch. Donald became a clergyman and a fierce critic of the Sutherland Clearances.

From the Mound, the mail coach carried on to Wick via a string of coastal villages starting with Golspie, a village created by and for the Duke and Duchess of Sutherland. On the 1,300-foot-high Ben Bhragaidh (aka Ben Braggie) overlooking the village is a gigantic monument bearing the statue of the 1st Duke of Sutherland (George Leveson-Gower, Marquess of Stafford). The statue of the 1st Duke may tower over the area, but there is a strong body of opinion that 'the Mannie', as it is derisively known, should be removed by one means or another. Considering the harsh and unfeeling clearances carried out in the early 1800s in the Sutherland name, the inscription on the monument that it was erected by 'a mourning and grateful tenantry' seems ironic. Golspie, like its near neighbour Brora, has a good stretch of sandy beach and a fine golf course, making them both attractive as resorts. Brora is noted, too, for its salmon fishing and its distillery, with the Clynelish malt whisky a connoisseur's favourite. Brora's imaginative heritage centre also attracts visitors.

Loch Fleet's Little Ferry was once well used, but little remains of the south side jetty, in contrast to the one at the other side at the village of Littleferry. (Author, 2018)

The railway line was added to the Mound in 1868 with a later branch to Dornoch sparking the rise of Dornoch as a golf and seaside resort. (Author's collection)

Indeed the number of heritage centres in Sutherland, and Caithness, is a notable feature of the area. These villages have a great deal in common, most notably because much of their growth and development resulted from the boom in the herring fishing industry that started in the early 1800s. Dunrobin Castle, the Duke of Sutherland's seat, is just north of Golspie and is a popular visitor attraction. From the shore the castle looks like a chateau transposed from the Loire Valley and plonked down in Sutherland. The 3rd Duke was a railway enthusiast of the first degree and made a large contribution to the cost of the extension of the Highland Railway into Sutherland. When Queen Victoria came to visit in 1872, she was surprised to find that, on reaching the station for Bonar Bridge (now Ardgay Station), the engine driver all the way from Inverness had been the 3rd Duke himself.

While Wick became the main centre for fish landings, other places, even tiny coves, were used to land herring. Helmsdale was one of the busiest with up to 250 boats fishing from there at its peak. The Sutherland Estate factors had new holdings laid out near Helmsdale for some of the crofters driven from their inland homes. These crofter-fishermen were expected to fish from the new estate-built Helmsdale harbour. Fishermen were also enticed over from the southern Moray Firth. The striking 'clearance memorial', which overlooks Helmsdale, depicts some of the emigrants who, after being forced out of their homes, were leaving for Canada with a mixture of anticipation and regret. A Canadian businessman, Helmsdale-born Dennis MacLeod, was the driving force behind the erection of this memorial and its twin at Winnipeg in Canada. The Telford Bridge of 1811 at Helmsdale is still in use but as a secondary road, a new road bridge

Golspie golf course is one of a number of fine courses on this stretch of coast. Ben Bhraggie stands out in the background with the 30-foot statue of the 1st Duke of Sutherland on its 76-foot pedestal. (Author's collection)

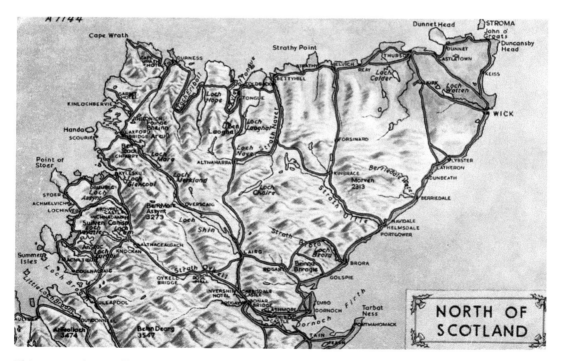

This postcard map illustrates the importance of the crossroads, those running in a north-west direction, for west and north coast villages like Ullapool and Tongue. (Author's collection)

having been built in 1972. The Bridge Inn, its extensive stables right opposite the inn, followed five years later. The traffic could not have been considerable as the Helmsdale toll keeper, like many others in this profession, needed an ancillary source of income. With very little money coming from tolls, he made his living from the sale of alcohol. Helmsdale's excellent Timespan Heritage Centre is a fount of information about these events and other aspects of local history.

A shore view of Dunrobin Castle. Ben Bhraggie, surmounted by the infamous statue to the first Duke of Sutherland, is on the right. (Author, 2014)

The Telford Bridge of 1811 at Helmsdale is still in use but a new road bridge of 1972 takes the main stream of traffic. The Bridge Inn followed in 1816. (Author 2019)

Transport history here in a nutshell: the Helmsdale change inn, the Bridge, at the top with opposite (top left) its stable. A garage with breakdown truck can also be seen, plus Timeline Heritage Centre (the yellow and white building). (Author, 2019)

The 'clearance memorial' at Helmsdale depicts emigrants who, cleared from their homes, were departing for Canada. Note on the hillside the meagre strips of land allocated to crofters in the 1800s (see also page 58). (Author, 2006)

5

Helmsdale to Thurso

The highway north from Helmsdale rises, with a few zig-zags, to nearly 700 feet in 4 miles. This is the Ord of Caithness, traversed by a road with a once notorious reputation. That was when the original road over the Ord ran perilously close to the cliff edge. Catherine Sinclair wrote in 1840 that the mail coach nowadays 'rattles down the whole descent of the Ord, scarcely deigning even to use a drag [a braking device].' Nevertheless, the notable nineteen-century English cyclist known as 'Nauticus' called the Ord dangerous and *The "Contour" Road Book of Scotland* (1898) warned cyclists in similar terms. Today's road is steep but poses no difficulty to modern cars. If there is one place to visit in this area, it would be Badbea Clearance village. A rough path from a car park a few miles along the A9 from Helmsdale leads to the ruins of this village built by evicted Highlanders. The terrain here is an unimaginably inhospitable one, but so desperate were these people for somewhere to live that they built homes using stones they cleared from the patches of rough ground they had been allocated. Returning to the highway, we come next to the Berriedale Braes, famous for its steep descents and tricky, hairpin bends. In stagecoach days Berriedale was a cocking station, a cock horse being a horse kept to help pull coaches up very steep hills. Road improvements here, it should be said, are currently underway. For Baddeley, writing in 1911, this tiny hamlet 'is the *bon mouche* of the route, and it is hardly possible to overpraise its beauty...'

North of the Ord we arrive at a series of villages that were built or expanded, usually by the local lairds, to exploit the fishing industry that began to develop rapidly in the course of the eighteenth century. This was a time when there was an enormous increase in the number of herring caught off the coast of Caithness. The herring boom, as it was termed, brought a new prosperity to the towns and villages of the east coast of Scotland. Dunbeath, Latheronwheel and Lybster were among the fishing stations of Sutherland and Caithness, which gained short-term prosperity as a result of the herring bonanza. Dunbeath-born author Neil M. Gunn's fine novel *The Silver Darlings* tells the story of this boom period, the silver darlings being the herrings that transformed the lives of people not only from Caithness but also from much further afield. The herring have gone from the nearby shores, but some of the physical remains of this time of explosive growth and development still survive, near empty harbours and derelict curing houses. One extraordinary survival from

At Badbea 'clearance village' we see the kind of ground that Highlanders cleared first for sheep and then deer had to try to till. Donald Sutherland of New Zealand erected the monument in memory of his father who had lived there. (Author, 2019)

During the shooting season hotels like the Portland Hotel at Lybster were very busy. Lord Portland owns estates in the area. (Author's collection)

these days are the Whaligoe Steps, a man-made stairway, leading down to a tiny cliff girt inlet that once housed twenty to thirty boats. This was a consequence, in the heyday of the herring fishery, of the shortage of landing places. At that time, the multitude of sailing drifters making their way back to port was a spectacle worth seeing. Today it is the 'sails' of the eighty-four giant wind turbines of the Beatrice Offshore Wind Farm, 13 km out to sea, that catch the eye. The power that they generate will replace that which is derived from another Beatrice, the oil platform of the same name that is visible from both sides of the Moray Firth. With production dating back to 1981, it is now deemed uneconomic and is to be dismantled.

As the Beatrice Offshore Wind Farm is operated and maintained from Wick harbour, the benefits to the town are considerable. The harbour at Wick was originally extended to cope with Wick being the epicentre of the Caithness herring boom. Wick developed rapidly including the building of a suburb-like new town – Pultneytown. The effects of the boom were felt all along the north coast with virtually every inlet being developed as a fishing 'station'. During the peak season hundreds of fishing boats arrived from the south coast of the Moray Firth and even further away. Staxigoe near Wick is a case in point with a large number of the small boats of the time based there. This haven was also, according to an 1846 report, 'much frequented by the enterprising Buckie fishermen, who are able to pass in and out with their large boats in any weather and at all times of the tide.' At the peak of the herring boom there were no fewer than twenty-one curing yards there. The introduction of even larger boats, however, heralded the end for Staxigoe and similar-sized harbours.

Herring gutters at Wick. Caitalise similar similar scenes were once commonplace at Staxigoe, Dunbeath and other east coast ports. (Author's collection)

The Simpson family found an alternative use for the old boat winch at the now little used Staxigoe Harbour. (Author, 1975)

As herring drifters increased in size so too did the need to further increase the size of Wick's harbour. Robert Louis Stevenson came to Wick as an apprentice engineer to assist with the harbour works that his father's firm was engaged in. In his essay *Education of an Engineer,* Stevenson described how in 1868 he had travelled to Wick in the Thurso coach, the railway having not reached that far north by that time. The coach top was crowded with Gaelic-speaking fishermen from Lewis – 'scarce anything but Gaelic had sounded in my ears'. Late at night as the coach neared the Pentland Firth he heard strange voices and 'the chatter of some foreign speech'. What Stevenson then saw at the roadside, in this most unlikely place, were 'two little dark-eyed, white-toothed Italian vagabonds, of twelve to fourteen years of age, one with a hurdy-gurdy, the other with a cage of white mice'. As the coach passed on, Stevenson was left to ponder on the circumstances that had brought them to this cold and rugged country. By then, for visitors from the south a stagecoach could now be regarded as one of the local curiosities, as we can see by this account from 1859 by Charles W. Weld: 'The scenery becomes wilder; cultivation rarer; and, to carry us still further from railways and civilisation, [he was on the road between Wick and Halkirk] here comes a genuine old mail-coach, guard and coachman resplendent in scarlet and gold lace, speeding past us at the rate of eleven miles an hour.'

Stevenson had mixed feelings about Wick, 'one of the meanest of man's towns'. Yet the sight of the fleet sailing silently out against a rising moon was one that he found to be

The herring drifter on this *c.* 1947 guidebook cover tells you immediately what Wick is about. For visitors to Wick there was a novel attraction at that time: occassional musical shows organised by the German prisoners in the POW camp at Watten (Camp 165). (Author's collection)

Duncansby Head, a short way from John o'Groats, is where Aldermaston nuclear scientists wanted to test a nuclear weapon in 1953. (Author's collection)

both strange and beautiful. Murray's 1894 *Handbook* was not complimentary either. Wick, it conceded, was a busy and thriving town, but it was 'not attractive to the tourist unless anxious for a lesson in gutting and curing herring.' Wick has a lot more going for it today, however, including, for the size of the town, one of the best heritage centres anywhere. By the 1930s Wick and the county's other main town Thurso were, if we can judge by the contemporary Caithness official guides, thoroughly modern and up-to-date with efforts being made to make them ideal holiday resorts. The stagecoach era was but a distant memory with both towns enjoying regular rail services to the south. The main Caithness hotels catered for the growing number of motorists tackling the long drive north. The number of long distance touring buses that were now arriving meant that Thurso's main hotel had to expand its bedroom and dining space and its streets had taken on, according to a 1930s guide, 'quite a cosmopolitan appearance'. By the 1930s you could also fly from Inverness to Thurso by Highland Airways, later Scottish Airways. Wick was served pre-war by Allied Airways from Aberdeen. There are still flights today but just to Wick not Thurso and from Aberdeen or Edinburgh not Inverness. Caithness attractions include the Castle of Mey with its royal connections and Dounreay nuclear power station – that is you want to see a nuclear plant being decommissioned. The castle is west of John o'Groats and Dounreay can be found on the coastal road west of Thurso, its unmistakable globe a prominent feature of the landscape.

The draw for many of the visitors to Caithness is, of course, John o'Groats, which some regard, albeit erroneously, as the most northerly point of the British mainland, the antithesis of Cornwall's Land's End. Although the most northerly point Dunnet Head lies

The availability of a summer-only John o'Groats passenger ferry to Orkney has greatly increased the number of day trips to Orkney. (Author, 2007)

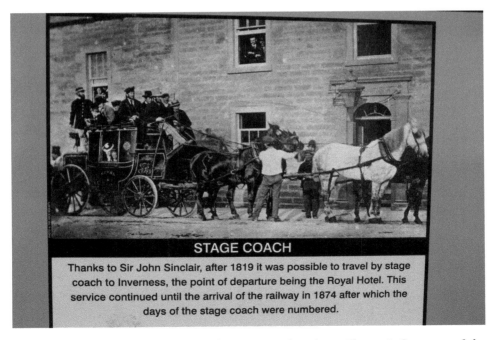

STAGE COACH

Thanks to Sir John Sinclair, after 1819 it was possible to travel by stage coach to Inverness, the point of departure being the Royal Hotel. This service continued until the arrival of the railway in 1874 after which the days of the stage coach were numbered.

This image of what is apparently the last stagecoach to leave Thurso is from one of the town's heritage display boards. (Author, 2019)

further west, John o'Groats impinged on the public imagination to such a degree that, for many years, it was classified as the terminal point for the A9. The modern A9, however, leaves the east coast at Latheron and goes direct to Thurso, thence to Scrabster, which is the main ferry port for Orkney. The other departure points are Gills Bay and John o'Groats, the latter in summer only.

The fascination with John o'Groats goes back a long time. As far back as 1803, Dorothy and William Wordsworth encountered a teacher in the Trossachs who was spending his vacation walking to John o'Groats. Making the 876-mile-long 'all-the-way' journey from Land's End to John o'Groats has a special appeal, despite Dunnet Head being the most northerly point. The first recorded all-the-way walker arrived in 1871, with countless others following suit. Some regarded it as a challenge just to get there, others insisted on employing an unusual form of transport like pushing a wheelbarrow or a pram. The growing popularity of cycling, from the 1880s, brought many touring cyclists to the Far North. From early days the supreme test for many cyclists was what they call the 'End-to-End'. Cycling had grown into a sport and leisure activity that enjoyed immense popularity with all sections of society. The safety bicycle equipped with the newly invented pneumatic tyres had displaced the penny-farthing. Long distance cycle touring became a

The Thurso toll house – now the Toll Gallery – was cannily sited to capture travellers coming to the town. (Author, 2019)

The River Naver enters the sea close to Bettyhill and it is not difficult to find a long stretch of a beach that you can have all to yourself. (Author, 2019)

craze with the middle classes, at least with those who had both the leisure time and the money to spare. Quite a few of the 50,000-strong Cyclists' Touring Club (CTC) came to the Highlands, a sufficient number at least for the Pentland Hotel in Thurso to display the CTC emblem – a flying-wheel – on its outside wall, thus signifying that CTC members could stay there on favourable terms.

The pioneer motorists were soon on the scene too, regarding this long-distance run north a suitable test for their very expensive vehicles. Some people, Henry Starley for instance, chose to go the other way south to Land's End. Having taken his car by train to Wick, he started by driving to John o'Groats and back, cheered on by a sizeable crowd of spectators. The next stage, the 38 miles drive to Helmsdale, horrified many, it being the Sabbath day. The first lady motorist, a nineteen-year-old girl from Kilkenny in Ireland, arrived in 1903, driving a Paisley-built Arrol-Johnston. She had had her first driving lessons just before the commencement of her journey. As with so many other similar 'triumphs', there may have been an element of a publicity stunt here, as her family were friendly with the car manufacturer's managing director. These Edwardian motorists could well have witnessed one of the last coaches still running – an ancient 'Defiance' that made a night-time journey carrying the mail from Thurso to Tongue. In 1875, according to Murray's *Handbook*, the mail car that linked Thurso to Tongue five times a week took around eight hours for the journey, with half an hour for breakfast at the Reay Inn. There were then two river ferries to be crossed by chain boats. The minibus serving this route, which this author travelled in in August 2019, ran only twice a week, but it did take considerably less time.

6

Thurso to Ullapool

We go from Caithness, a county where hills are the exception, to Sutherland – the diametric opposite. Sutherland, the Southland to the Norsemen, is rugged and wild and until the 1830s had few roads suitable for carriages. It was around then that the Sutherland Estate started to carry out much needed road improvements. Nevertheless, progress was slow and even into the Edwardian era cyclists were being warned about the difficulties of cycling in the far north-west. Black's *Shilling Guide* (1906 edition) advised cyclists who, after reaching John o'Groats, wanted to go next to Fort William just to take the train back to Inverness. They could then get to Fort William by cycling along the canal path. Baddeley's 1911 *Guide* was not so dismissive, but warned: 'Cyclists who undertake a ride round the North of Scotland will find their work cut out for them.' Even today, much of the road along the top of Scotland is narrow single-track road with passing places. There was no west coast highway equivalent to the Great North Road. The mountainous terrain with numerous rivers and long sea lochs slicing far into the interior made such a north to south highway out of the question until comparatively recent times. For the people of the west, the sea was the great highway, steamships substituting for stagecoaches and railways.

Nowadays Sutherland's lochs and mountains are not a deterrent but the attraction for many tourists. Along the north coast of Sutherland, and Caithness too, there are many places with spectacular cliff scenery and beautiful beaches. Of the villages one of the largest is the spread-out settlement of Bettyhill where the River Naver goes into the sea. Bettyhill was the destination for many of the Countess of Sutherland's crofters when they were cleared from Strathnaver to make way for sheep farms. The Strathnaver Museum in the former parish kirk explains in a measured way the story of these clearances. It was in that very kirk that Reverend David Mackenzie read out the eviction notices that were issued to the Strathnaver crofters in those dreadful years from 1814 to 1819. Plans are underway now to enlarge the building and enhance the displays and facilities for research. Bettyhill enjoys the benefit too of a well-stocked shop, which is something that nowadays is sadly lacking in many other Highland villages. Tourists, and more importantly the locals, often have to drive a long way to find not just a shop but also fuel for their vehicles.

ANDREW PATERSON   TONGUE HOTEL. SUTHERLAND   INVERNESS

Baddeley in 1911 described the Tongue Hotel as deservedly a favourite and, judging by this 1920s postcard, it continued to be. (Author's collection)

Castle Varrich or Caisteal Bharraich in Gaelic is easily accessible from Tongue. Ben Hope, the most northerly Munro, looms in the background, its summit shrouded in cloud. (Author, 2019)

At Durness we see one of the north coast's many fine beaches. In the background, we can see a typical example of how the land allocated to crofters was divided into small strips (see also p. 46). (Author's collection)

Tongue, the next settlement of any size after Bettyhill, was described in Murray's 1895 *Handbook* 'as a charming place, with beautiful sea-views and to the south a grand outline of 'the four-headed Ben Laoghal (aka Loyal) in sight'. Instead of a ferry across the Kyle of Tongue, there is a causeway and bridge, the former built in 1971 with no consideration given to walkers or cyclists. Pedestrians coming from the village cross at their peril until the sidewalk on the bridge section is reached. For passing tourists, there are public toilets, one shop, a few B&Bs, two hotels, and a hostel. If plans to build a spaceport on the nearby A'Mhoine peninsula are realised, the economy of Tongue and the whole area will be transformed.

In the late 1800s pedestrians walking the 20 miles from Tongue to Durness had three ferries to take – the first over the Kyle of Tongue and then the second over the River Hope. The last of the three ferries was based at Heilim Inn on the east side of Loch Eriboll. Missing it meant walking an extra 10 miles. In his book *The Travels of Tramp Royal* (1932) Matt Marshall wrote amusingly of the prolonged procedure involved in getting this ferry, an enormous sailing boat, ready for use. In 1911 Baddeley described how lairds could exercise their influence. Years earlier, he relates, the Heilim Inn had lost its licence as there were stone quarries nearby and, at the landowner's behest, the inn had its licence taken away 'to save the quarrymen from temptation'. In the two world wars the Royal Navy made good use of the sheltered, deep anchorage that Loch Eriboll provided. When the surviving German U-boats surrendered at the end of the Second World War, no fewer than thirty-five of them made their way into Loch Eriboll.

The beaches and bird life attract many visitors to Durness, the largest settlement in the far north. The base rock being limestone means the land is more fertile than usual in the Highlands. With a hostel and other accommodation, hikers find it a good base for visiting Cape Wrath and for climbing Ben Hope, Scotland's most northerly Munro. The Smoo Cave is worth a visit and tourists may have the unusual experience of a short boat trip into the depths of the cave. 'Nauticus', who in 1882 was cycling round Scotland on a tricycle, found the ten shillings charge too steep so he skipped it. Durness, too, lays claim to the accolade of most northerly mainland golf course, and visitors looking to buy gifts will find much on offer at the nearby Balnakeil Craft Village.

Access to Cape Wrath, the north-west tip of the British mainland, is by a small passenger ferry across the Kyle of Durness. In 1927, according to Muirhead's *Blue Guide*, the ferryman charged 25 shillings to carry visitors to the lighthouse in his dog cart. Nowadays it is a minibus that operates in the summer months. The amenities at the lighthouse are few but include an all-year-round small café and a Mountain Bothies Association bothy. Cape Wrath's name derives from the Old Norse word hvarf, which means a turning point. For the Norsemen it was the turning point where the longships turned south towards the rich spoils to be seized from defenceless monasteries like Iona. Though no longer manned, the 400-feet-high lighthouse still casts a friendly warning beam. Visitors need to be aware that live firing exercises are sometimes held on Ministry of Defence-owned land in the area.

Just as Cape Wrath is the mariners' turning point, so Durness is ours. Heading south now we come to Rhiconich, where the road to the west, the B807, leads to Kinlochbervie, which, like Scrabster on the north coast, has become a significant port for landing fish. East coast and continental fishermen as well as west coasters use Kinlochbervie as a convenient place to land their catches. In consequence, massive refrigerated trucks loaded with fish may be encountered on the roads, many of them bound for continental markets.

The next landmark is Laxford Bridge, which crosses the River Laxford – another famous salmon river emanating from the loch of the same name. Loch Laxford means salmon fiord in Old Norse. The area surrounding Laxford Bridge is part of the Reay Forest, which formerly belonged to Lord Reay, hereditary chieftain of the Clan Mackay. In 1829 the Reay Forest was purchased by the Countess of Sutherland (Duchess from 1833), adding to an already enormous estate. By the end of the nineteenth century vast areas of the Highlands and Islands had been turned into 'deer forests'. This kind of Highland forest usually has very few trees, it being first and foremost a sporting estate. In other parts of the Highlands crofting land and sheep farms were converted into stalking estates. A Ross-shire minister, giving evidence to the Crofters' Commission, lamented how it was possible – this was in the early 1880s – to walk from one side of Ross-shire to the other 'without putting a foot on anything but deer forest, practically from sea to sea'.

Though few people live there, Laxford Bridge is important as the cut-off point for Lairg, which is the railhead for the north-west. Lairg was where in the nineteenth century travellers transferred from the train to the mail coach, and in the twentieth century from train to mail bus. The change over from horse-drawn vehicle to motor bus took place very quickly. According to Black's 1907 *Guide*, 'public motors' were now operating from Lairg to Lochinver, Tongue and Scourie. However, travellers to Durness were less fortunate as they had a motor, the Scourie one, only as far as Laxford. From there it was back to horse transport for the rest of the journey.

The road from Laxford Bridge to Lairg was 'a destitution road' built during the Highland potato famine of 1846/7. Work on this road and others like it provided crofters with the basic means of survival. Since payment was in the form of food, such roads were also known as 'meal roads'. In 1882 'Nauticus' found the roads in the north, as generally elsewhere in Scotland, excellent with a firm gravel surface which at that time was the standard everywhere. In this area the roads were toll-free as there wasn't sufficient traffic to make it worthwhile. Road works, and the inevitable subsequent repairs, still had to be paid for. In this county, therefore, tenant-farmers and householders, instead of being obliged to spend valuable time working on the roads, were allowed to substitute a money payment. Householders who had fallen behind with their road fund payments or rents could also pay their arrears by stone breaking and other work on the roads. The cross-country road from Lochinver to Golspie via Ledmore and Oykel Bridge had priority because Golspie with Dunrobin Castle on its doorstep was the administrative 'capital' of the Sutherland family's empire, which at that time was the largest private estate in Western Europe.

SCOURIE VILLAGE, SUTHERLANDSHIRE.

The houses in Scourie, as in many Highland villages, are spread over a sizeable area with little in the way of discernible planning. (Author's collection)

THE FERRY AND LOCH GLENDHU (ASSYNT).

The Royal Scottish Automobile Club met the cost of a motorised car ferry for Kylesku. One car, as seen here on a Raphael Tuck postcard, was its maximum load. (Author's collection)

The inns and hotels in the north-west, as elsewhere in the Highlands, were always popular with anglers, and the hotel in Scourie was no exception. In 1875 it was described as an inn that was comfortable and the charges moderate. By 1911 it was being called a hotel, the kind of change in nomenclature that was happening in most places. According to Baddeley's 1911 *Guide*, Scourie Hotel, though small, was exceptionally pleasant with good fishing, with some boats available free of use for their guests on five specified lochs. A favourite boat excursion in this area, then and now, is to see the bird life on nearby Handa Island – nowadays a nature reserve owned by the Scottish Wild Life Trust.

While the Victorian-age tourists to Sutherland included naturalists, geologists and other lovers of wild places, it is probably true that in the past most of those who ventured into the far north were there to shoot and fish. To quote the eminent historian C. J. Smout: 'More men came to kill in the wilderness than to admire it.' Quite a few of them were on so-called 'reading parties', theoretically preparing for Oxford or Cambridge exams. Lord Cockburn was sceptical about the amount of Greek imbibed by such parties 'but they can do nothing better for their minds and bodies than breathe such air...' Other travellers complained that such groups often monopolised the few private rooms in what were usually tiny inns. All the Kylesku Inn could provide in those days, according to 'Nauticus', was 'a shake-down to two or three travellers'.

Conscious of their prestige, the Victorian landowners began to upgrade and enlarge the inns on their estates. In later decades, some landowners adopted a different policy. Fearing that mountaineers and ramblers were encroaching on their sporting fiefdoms, some owners secured the closure of inns frequented by the hill-walking fraternity. In those parts of the Highlands where sporting estates predominated it therefore became difficult to find accommodation. Landowners closed inns on their land or used their power and status to deprive them of licences, thus rendering them unprofitable as seems to have been the case with Heilim Inn at Loch Eriboll. Ernest Baker, writing in 1932, argued that owners had turned large parts of the Highlands 'into a solitude', where a few rich men bring their friends to shoot and fish. The establishment in 1933 of the Scottish Youth Hostel Association (SYHA), which had the backing of some well-disposed lairds, did bring some improvement for Wester Ross at least. North of Ullapool, however, as B. H. Humble writing observed in 1936, it was different: 'walkers are seldom seen . . . hotels are far apart and rather expensive for most walkers.'

It is likely that the sportsmen that 'Nauticus' met at different hotels in the north-west had travelled by train to Lairg and then the rest of the way by mail coach or hired gig. The alternative was to go by sea to Lochinver and then get a hire from there. Only a few hardy pedestrians and cyclists emulated 'Nauticus' by making their own way to the region. Baddeley's 1911 *Guide* provided a number of recommended 'tours' for cyclists, but with one exception omitted the north-west Highlands 'because in that part of the country a cycle is a nuisance to the rider'. By the early twentieth century, a few private motorists had begun to make their way north, though they found the frequent recourse to ferries a severe drawback. Annoyed with the delays at Kylesku ferry, the wealthy members of the Royal Scottish Automobile Club took the matter into their own hands, commissioning a motor

The ferry *Maid of Kylesku* remained in service until 1976, latterly only in a relief capacity. It is still at Kylesku, but beached and abandoned. (Author, 2019)

ferry in 1926. Unusually for the Highlands it operated a Sunday service and was free, a tradition maintained by Sutherland County Council when it took over the service in 1948. Although Sutherland County Council provided a new ferry, the *Maid of Kylesku*, in 1952, the Kylestrome to Kylesku crossing remained a bottleneck for many years. The boats were replaced in 1984 by the present much-admired bridge.

Once across the Kylesku Bridge we enter a landscape studded with lochans and mountains like Suilven and Cul Mor, which rise steeply and dramatically out of the surrounding moorland. This is Assynt, noted for its geology. One mile south of Kylesku Bridge at Unapool, we can learn all about the local geology at a craft shop-cum-café called the Rock Stop and much more too at the free visitor centre at Knockan Crag south of Inchnadamph. In 1993 Assynt hit the headlines when the Assynt Crofters' Trust made the first community buyout in Scotland of a private estate, the North Assynt Estate. Travellers following the North Coast 500 can take the B869 road to Lochinver via Drumbeg and Stoer. Although the views are spectacular and there are popular camping sites at Clachtoll and Achmelvich, visitors need to be aware that it is a narrow, winding road with many steep, blind bends, and Lochinver can be more easily accessed by a good road from Skiag Bridge. In Victorian times the majority of visitors to Lochinver came by sea, mostly by the twice-weekly steamer from Glasgow. The very rich, however, travelled in style in their own steam yachts. In consequence, by the early 1900s Lochinver had developed into 'a favourite resort of all classes of tourists'. In those days 'all classes' certainly did not include the working class who were not likely to have stayed in the 'first-class' Culag Hotel, built originally for the Duke of Sutherland as his west coast Marine Lodge.

The Culag Hotel in Lochinver with two of Sutherland's most distinctive mountains, Canisp (left) and Suilven (right), in the background. (Author's collection)

Ardvreck Castle, a former stronghold of the Macleods of Assynt, is located by Loch Assynt. In 1650 the Marquis of Montrose was held prisoner there before being taken south for execution. (Author, 2019)

The author seeing Suilven from a different angle. This view was taken from Fionn Loch in the Inverpolly National Nature Reserve, south-east of Lochinver. (Author, 2016)

The Corbett Cul Mor is another of the iconic Assynt peaks, also seen from the vicinity of Fionn Loch. (Author, 2016)

A short distance from Skiag Bridge we arrive at Inchnadamph, a mecca for fishermen, geologists and cavers. This district is famous for its disappearing river and its limestone caves including the Uamh an Claonaite, the longest cave in Scotland. Inchnadamph Hotel, was a stop over for 'Nauticus' when cycling north from Ullapool. He stayed long enough to visit Glean Dubh (the Dark Glen) to see the 'disappearing' River Traligill and to attend the local kirk, where the service was in Gaelic, which of course he could not understand. On the way south from Inchdamph to Ullapool we pass a number of crofting townships, the most notable being Elphin and Knockan. Elphin was one place where the crofters successfully thwarted an attempt to evict them. When the sheriff officer arrived, the local women wrestled him to the ground, seized the summonses and burnt them. Perhaps conscious of the bad publicity previously engendered by the Kildonan Clearances, the Sutherland Estate managers stopped the removals.

Ullapool differs from most Highland villages inasmuch as it is laid out in systematic form on the north side of Loch Broom. This is because it was a planned village, like Wick's Pulteneytown, founded in 1788 and built to a plan designed by Thomas Telford. Murray's 1875 *Handbook* was hardly enthusiastic, however – 'a large, dreary fishing village'. The herring fishery, it went on to say, had utterly died away, and this

This part of the Uamh an Claonaite cave system in Assynt can only be reached by experienced cave divers. (Fraser Simpson, 1998)

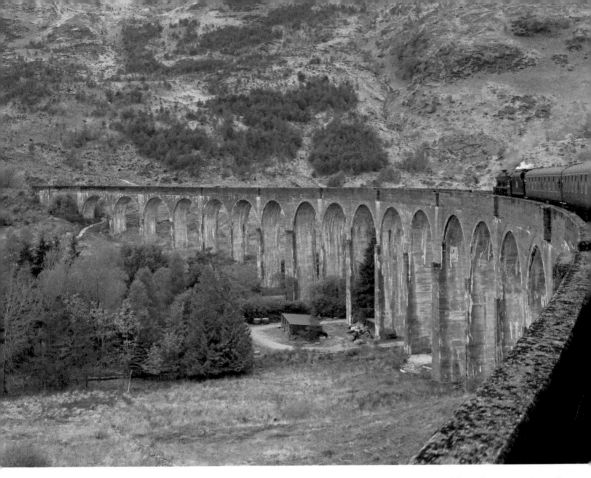

The Glenfinnan Railway Viaduct is familiar to viewers of the Harry Potter films, but it is also of considerable engineering and historical interest. (Author, 2017)

presumably explained the many roofless and half-ruined houses. Though created as a fishing centre, it was as a tourist resort that Ullapool eventually prospered. There are a variety of shops and galleries, an excellent museum and a regular ferry to Stornoway. They are keen on festivals in Ullapool and, with two good bookshops, one, of course, is a book festival.

Leaving Ullapool we follow the A835 to Braemore Junction. The spectacular Corrieshalloch Gorge is close to the junction and worth seeing. Turning west at Braemore we continue on the A832, which takes us to Gairloch via Dundonell and Aultbea. There is a lot to see and admire in this area, especially around Gruinard Bay. Although located in this most beautiful corner of the Highlands, little Gruinard Island was chosen as the location for a deadly experiment in germ warfare during the Second World War. Anthrax was tested there for use in possible biological warfare. It took nearly fifty years for the island to be declared safe. Carrying on south, we come to Loch Ewe, which had a more positive wartime role to play as a convoy assembly anchorage. A must-visit site here are the marvellous Inverewe Gardens, now in the care of the National Trust for Scotland. Gairloch

Ullapool viewed from above reveals its regular street layout. The hill on the far side of Loch Broom is Beinn Ghobhlach. (Author, 2016)

too has a long history as a tourists' favourite. Its attractions include a good beach and an excellent museum located in what was the operations centre for the wartime anti-aircraft batteries. Still on the A832, we continue past one of the most famous and beautiful of Scotland's lochs, Loch Maree. From 1883 to 1911 tourists coming from Achnasheen Railway Station could travel to Gairloch via Loch Maree, travelling by coaches to and from the loch and on the loch by a little steamboat, the SS *Mabel* – today we would call it an integrated service. A glorified tea-kettle was one traveller's unkind comment on this vessel. From Loch Maree to Kinlochewe, which, though small, has most of the essentials that tourists look for in a Highland village – namely a shop, toilets, petrol station and an old established hotel. Kinlochewe is strategically positioned at the turn-off for Torridon and close to the Ben Eighe National Nature Reserve. This area is a hill walkers' mecca, one worth returning to again and again as this writer has done. My favourite place to stay was the old hostel at Inveralligin on the north side of Loch Torridon. It was possible to get there by ferry, as I once did, by phoning the warden, Mr Macdonald – phone number Alligin 1. Mr Macdonald filled many roles, one being the ferryman. The replacement

In the Second World War Gairloch Hotel was a military hospital. It was built in 1872 to cater for tourists arriving mainly by steamer. (Author, 2019)

Torridon Hostel is a striking piece of architecture, but lacks the character, and discomfort it must be admitted, of the old one.

Travellers today enjoy the benefit of a road from Shieldaig that goes round the coast of the Applecross peninsula to the main village, passing a number of largely deserted settlements on the way. Writing in the late 1940s, Daphne Pochin Mould came across one 'a half deserted hamlet' called Lonbain. There were still a few inhabited houses, but the fields were neglected and ruin was everywhere. The reason for its decay was the absence of a road to the outside world. In 1957 a friend and I hiked along that track heading for Lonbain, where the former schoolhouse had been converted into a very basic youth hostel. Though the county council maintained the track, it was not wide enough for a motor vehicle. The larger villages of Shieldaig and Applecross (strictly speaking the village name is the Street) were served by roads, although in the latter case one with severe drawbacks. In 1816 Shieldaig had been connected to the outside world by a parliamentary road to Lochcarron; Applecross 'village' was connected to Lochcarron by the Bealach na Bo road

The view to the south from the Applecross road. The road was built in 1826. (Author, 2016)

ten years later. The townships in between had to make do with a simple path. The coastal townships, had to wait until 1976. By that time most of the few remaining inhabitants had gone, sadly a too familiar a story, and one that has been repeated all over the Highlands. The plea for a road to these coastal townships went back a long way. In 1883 when the Crofters' Commission was taking evidence from the Highland crofters, the principal complaint of the folk from that part of the Applecross peninsula was not rent levels, but the lack of a road to serve their townships. Once a road was built, some of the dwellings were restored and reoccupied, including the former youth hostel.

If Shieldaig is the northern gateway to the Applecross peninsula, Lochcarron, which borders the loch of the same name, is the southern, and, like Shieldaig, a lovely place. When Robert Southey came to Lochcarron in 1819 (he was accompanying Thomas Telford on a tour of the area roadworks) it was called Jeantown. Southey described it as the largest place in West Ross 'a large but populous village, chiefly or wholly inhabited by fishermen.' Lochcarron and Shieldaig are white-washed, neat and possibly sober villages – well, Shieldaig has a Temperance Brae. Once we pass Loch Kishorn (another picturesque spot despite a construction yard), it is more or less uphill until we reach the summit of the Bealach na

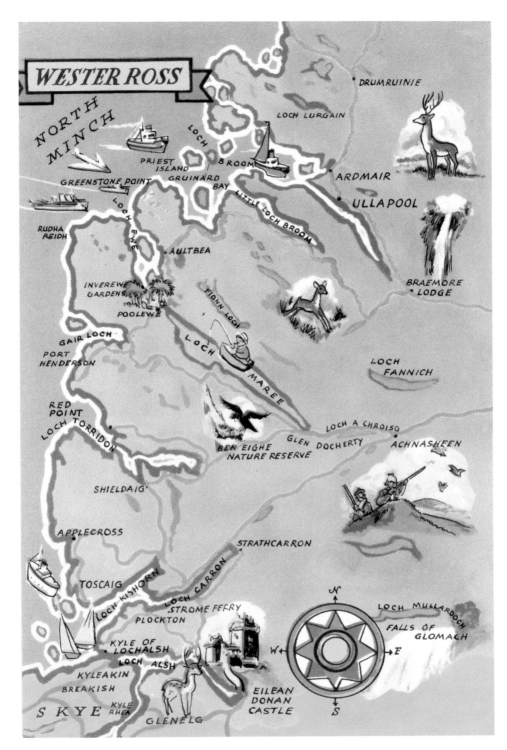

This postcard map predates the building of the coastal road from Shieldaig to Applecross via Lonbain. (Author's collection)

After a road was built on the south side of Loch Carron, the once busy Strome Ferry became redundant – likewise the adjacent hotel. (Author's collection)

Plockton always looks lovely, whether in summer or, as we see here, in winter. (Author, 2013)

Bo – aka Pass of the Cattle at 2,050 feet. But please don't attempt to drive a large campervan over the Bealach in snow and ice, or indeed in any conditions! Take the other road round the coast. The 'village' of Applecross has a community-owned petrol station, a wonderful pub and a lot more beside. The estate is owned by the Applecross Trust, which is run by seven people – none of whom live in Applecross!

From Lochcarron, the North Coast 500 purists will head back towards Inverness while we continue round the south side of Loch Carron, with more splendid views still to come. The south road is comparatively new compared to many in the Highlands, dating back just to 1970. That explains why Stromeferry has a sign that perplexes many travellers. It reads 'Stromeferry (No Ferry)!' Never say never though – in 2012 a ferry service had to be reintroduced for a spell following a major road blockage. After Stromeferry take a minor road, still on the north side of the Loch Carron, to Plockton, yet another village gem. It has an inn with live traditional music, a railway station and an airport. You won't find

The airfield at Plockton is of use to, as here, employees of the Northern Lighthouse Board, and other public bodies. (Author, 2017)

A shinty match near Dornie. Shinty features highly in Highland sporting culture. (Author, 2017)

an international flight at the airport, though, or a control tower – or even any staff. But, if you chance to need it, aviation fuel is available there, namely Jet A1 (aka paraffin). It is self-service with an honesty box.

The road south from Stromeferry joins the A87, which, if you then go further west, takes you to Kyle of Lochalsh and the glories of Skye. On this occasion we turn east towards Dornie and Loch Duich coming to a castle that until the twentieth century was a ruin. Held by a pro-Jacobite force (mainly Spanish) during the 1719 Rising, the castle was bombarded by British government frigates and left a ruin. Superlatively restored, the image of this most picturesque castle ornaments many a shortbread tin, even rivalling Bonnie Prince Charlie for that honour. Dornie nearby is another bonnie village unfortunately, or perhaps fortunately for the residents, bypassed when Loch Long was bridged in 1940. From Dornie to Shiel Bridge we drive, or cycle, along Loch Duich, the mountains known as the Five Sisters of Kintail providing a wonderful backdrop. From Shiel Bridge south to Loch Cluanie we follow the line of Telford's road. Glen Shiel is another area beloved by hill walkers. There are numerous Munros (hills over 3,000 feet) on both sides of the glen, seven of which are on the south side on one long ridge. Within the glen itself, the lonely Cluanie

Inn – the bar especially – is a long-standing favourite with hill walkers. Glen Shiel was the scene of the battle that brought the 1719 Jacobite Rising to an end. Their defeat came at the narrow part of the pass. It was the Spanish government that, on this occasion, provided the supporting troops, but the force sent was far too small, a mere 300 men. They left their mark inasmuch as one of the Glen Shiel hills is the Sgurr nam Spainteach (aka the Peak of the Spaniards).

From Cluanie Inn to Invergarry, once again we are on a 'new' road, the former highway having been sacrificed to meet the post-war demand for hydro-electric power. Lochs were being dammed all over the Highlands, and these included Lochs Loyne and Garry. The Loch Garry viewpoint on the 'new' road is a favourite halt, as the loch stretched out below resembles a map of Scotland. At Invergarry, a neat and tidy village, we leave the A87 and join the A82, the Inverness to Glasgow road. The road follows the line of the Great Glen Fault, a geological rift caused by the collision of tectonic plates. Be reassured, occasional minor tremors apart, the fault is inactive. The glen was subsequently eroded by glaciers thus allowing the formation of the three lochs of the Great Glen – Loch Ness, Loch Oich and Loch Lochy, all links on the Caledonian Canal. The road through the Great Glen was rebuilt as part of the major road reconstruction of the interwar years. As usual General Wade had been there first. Recognising the key importance of Inverness at one end of the glen and Fort William at the other, the General commenced his road building programme by linking the two fortresses. His route differed from today's; between Inverness and Fort Augustus, his road was built on the south side of Loch Ness, whereas the new road of the 1930s was carved out on the north side. Completed in 1934, the new highway was opened by the then Minister of Transport Leslie Hore-Belisha, who gave his name to the Belisha Beacons that adorn our streets. Wider roads with fewer bends meant faster traffic, one immediate consequence being that the bus time between Inverness and Fort William was reduced by one hour. The first bus on this route was in 1911 and operated by MacBrayne. Thomas Telford's Caledonian Canal runs parallel to the road. We join the highway on the north side of Loch Oich before crossing to the south side at the Laggan Locks. In 1824 a steamboat, the *Ben Nevis*, started a service between Glasgow and Inverness via the Crinan and Caledonian canals, thus commencing a long period when the canal was the main artery of communication between Inverness and Fort William. Until 1894 when the railway came, most visitors to 'The Fort' were waterborne, arriving either by sea or via the Caledonian Canal. The steamship service ceased with the outbreak of war in 1939. After the war, it was realised that, except for tourist traffic, passenger steamers could not compete with the buses, so there was no resumption.

Continuing by Loch Lochy en route to Fort William, a photo stop at the impressive Commando Memorial is recommended. It was in the testing country hereabouts that the Commando troops did much of their initial training during the Second World War. A short distance from here we arrive at Spean Bridge, another popular spot for a short break. It is also the junction of the A86 to Badenoch and Strathspey, on the one hand, and Dalwhinnie and the A9 on the other. Nearing Fort William we come to the Nevis Range multi-sports centre, which is not on Ben Nevis as the name might suggest, but on the nearly as high Aonach Mor. Nevertheless you can take a ride on a mountain gondola up to around 2,000 feet. An alternative is go mountain biking on a variety of

THE FORD CAR
(STANDARD MODEL CHASSIS)
ON BEN NEVIS.

'Motor Car on Ben Nevis'
most dangerous corner

Henry Alexander in a Ford Model T descending Ben Nevis in 1911 on the pony track built to serve the observatory. Pedestrians paid a toll to use the path. (Author's collection)

The path by the Caledonian Canal at Fort William is popular with ramblers and cyclists. The shoulder of the Munro Carn Mor Dearg, which can be an alternative route to Ben Nevis, is prominent in the background. (Author, 2019)

trails. Just before reaching Fort William, a short diversion to see the most impressive set of canal locks at Banavie, otherwise known as Neptune's Staircase, is highly recommended, as is a visit to the battle-scarred Inverlochy Castle. A stronghold of the locally dominant Comyn family, it is an unusual example as this castle remains largely as it was when built in the 1200s.

Fort William gets its name from a seventeenth-century fort whose Gaelic name, An Gearasdan, translates as The Garrison, and that name tells that it was a fortification erected by occupation forces, originally Cromwell's troopers. In the eighteenth century the fort was rebuilt by Hanoverian forces to stem the local Jacobite threat. Though not the bonniest of towns, the scenery round about is incomparable and that lets the townsfolk combine tourism and industry. Having Ben Nevis, the highest mountain in Britain, on the doorstep is a major asset, but the Fort William area has many other features that attract sporty types and other visitors. A memorable outing is a trip to Mallaig either by road or by rail. With the latter, there is the option of travelling in the Jacobite steam train to Mallaig during the

The steamer King George V approaching Fort William on an excursion from Oban in 1951. Three Maudslay buses await the passengers. (Author's collection)

The Telford-age 'Road to the Isles' – Fort William to Mallaig by Glenfinnan. A solitary car on a lonely stretch of road must be the photographer's. (Author's collection)

tourist season and that trip incorporates the spectacular Glenfinnan Railway Viaduct. The town's West Highland Museum is worth a visit. Outside the museum there is a bronze sculpture of a Ford Model T car and its driver, Edinburgh Ford dealer Henry Alexander, who drove a Model T to the top of Ben Nevis in May 1911. Films show that it was not without some assistance (see image on p. 76).

For many people today, Fort William is also the end, or start, point of a highly popular long-distance walking route – the West Highland Way. Opened in 1980, it extends from Milngavie near Glasgow to Fort William. It is reckoned that around 36,000 people complete the route each year – all 96 miles/154 km of it. Most elect to finish in Fort William. The Way embraces traditional paths and drove roads, parts of the old military road, and sections of Telford's early ninteenth-century reconstruction. Whether walking on the West Highland Way or cycling or motoring on the present highway, we follow in the steps of those who have carved out a path for us – the drovers and the engineers, both military and civilian.

7

Fort William to Tyndrum

In the era of Telford, the traditional route south from Fort William was, at certain times of the year, an extremely busy one, but as on the Great North Road the traffic was mostly of a four-legged nature. With cattle rearing traditionally the mainstay of the Highland economy, large droves of cattle were despatched to southern markets. Herds of cattle and flocks of sheep came from all parts of the north-west Highlands and Islands with many of them meeting at Kingshouse, just south of Glencoe, and from there going on to the trysts, initially at Crieff and then mainly at Falkirk. The passage of countless thousands of cattle and sheep had created a road of sorts, and this was often the line selected by the military engineers. Even after the rebellious Jacobite clans had been crushed at Culloden in 1746, the Hanoverian army of occupation continued with its road building programme. One priority for Major Caulfeild was the construction of a military road linking Fort William to the army's Lowland stronghold at Stirling Castle. Commencing in 1748 the road, which went via Tyndrum and Callander, was finished five years later. As with the other military roads, small work parties continued with repairs and maintenance until 1790.

The military engineers did not always choose their routes wisely – the road from Fort William to Altnafeidh by the Devil's Staircase being one example of this. It was abandoned early on – in 1785 – in favour of a new road. The Devil's Staircase, however, was given new life when in 1980 it became part of the West Highland Way. Thomas Pennant in 1774 considered the military roads to be excellent, but the last section to Fort William had been 'very injudiciously planned'. It was his opinion that it would have been better to follow the track used by the local people – in other words, the drovers. Telford's replacement road did just that by going from Fort William along the coast by Loch Linnhe, passing the Corran Ferry site on the way. An attractive diversion here would be to cross the ferry to Ardgour and thence to Moidart – Prince Charlie country – or to the most westerly point of the British mainland, Ardnamurchan Point. Our route, though, continues through Onich to Ballachulish at the head of Loch Leven, a particularly lovely stretch of road. The main ferry across Loch Leven was here at the mouth of the loch. Ballachulish means 'the village by the narrows' in Gaelic, and originally just referred to the settlement on the north side. Ferry delays and proximity to tourist-magnet Glencoe meant that hotels on both sides of the loch prospered. Henry Alexander driving up Ben Nevis was a sign of the times and in the following year, 1912, with more vehicles on the road a motorised turntable vessel was introduced to the ferry here. However, it could only carry one vehicle at a time.

By 1975, when the Ballachulish Bridge was completed, the ferry boats were carrying over 200,000 passengers a year. There are the remains of another pier west of the bridge, which was used by MacBrayne's steamers on the Oban to Fort William run to disembark passengers who wished to see Glencoe. Horse-drawn coaches waited at the pier for the steamer's arrival and 'ample time' was allowed for this spectacular trip. Tourists could sit back and, if visibility allowed, enjoy the scenery, all the while learning about Glencoe's bloody history – clan rivalries and the Massacre of Glencoe, the Appin murder and the subsequent judicial murder of James Stewart, aka James of the Glen. James Stewart had been falsely accused of the murder of hated clan enemy Colin Campbell. Found guilty by a packed Campbell jury, James was hanged from a gibbet overlooking the ferry and his skeleton was left hanging there for years as a dreadful warning. The mystery of who actually killed Colin Campbell is one that has puzzled many over the generations. Robert Louis Stevenson's splendid novel *Kidnapped* revolves round this event and its aftermath.

The Ballachulish Ferry near the mouth of Loch Leven, once a notorious bottleneck, continued in use until midnight on 23 December 1975. The new bridge opened just after midnight on Christmas Eve. On the south side of the loch we see the Ballachulish Hotel. (Author's collection).

The Glencoe Hotel in the 1930s. At the roadside an AA box and the patrolman's motorbike and sidecar can be seen. (Author's collection)

Come the motor age and more tourists came to Glencoe by car and bus. MacBrayne's steamers now stopped at Kentallan, further south on the coast road to Oban instead of Ballachulish with motor coaches conveying disembarked passengers to Glencoe from there. Two miles further on from the bridge there is another and larger Ballachulish village. The first dwellings here were built for the employees at the large slate quarries that were worked here from 1692 to 1955. There are now short scenic walks with interpretation boards in the quarries. Glencoe village is another attractive spot that also has fine walks and an interesting museum.

The Pass of Glencoe has an unjustifiable reputation as savage, dark and gloomy, largely because of the Massacre which took place here on 13 February 1692. For Charles Dickens, it was perfectly terrible, 'an awful place'. The author of *Scotland for the Motorist* (1928 edition) endorsed this view while recognising 'perhaps nowhere in Scotland is the majesty of the mountains more forcibly impressed on one's mind than at the heart of the Glen.' Strangely for a book published for the AA there was little about the condition of the road, although the accompanying photograph shows an extremely stony surface. AA members were warned, however, to take great care when descending the series of 'corkscrews' into the glen beneath. Over the centuries, the first place of shelter, after emerging from the glen, was the Kingshouse Inn, now Hotel. This inn had begun, as the name suggests, as a place of shelter and refreshment for the king's men, the soldiers working on and maintaining the King's Highway. The section of the military road south from the Kingshouse Inn to Bridge of Orchy was, however, another that had been badly chosen, and it had to be replaced. Telford once more built his road by more or less following the old drovers' route. By 1843 the new road was good enough for the operation of a coach service between Fort William and the north end of Loch Lomond. From there travellers could proceed to Balloch by loch steamer, and thence to Glasgow. In 1859 Charles Weld travelled in the Loch Lomond coach, 'a huge van-like' vehicle, on what was its last trip of the season. That proved to be an unforgettable experience, especially as the coachman was plied with whisky at each halt. Weld had elected to walk through Glencoe, but nevertheless he managed to arrive at the King's House Inn, as it was then, long before the coach. The horses were then galloped downhill from the Blackmount to Tyndrum 'scattering, to the dismay of their shepherds, thousands of sheep that were being driven to the Falkirk cattle Tryst, and which whitened the road for many miles.' Eighteen years earlier, Charles Dickens had gone in the other direction, uphill 'over a place called the Black-Mount ... to a lone public house called the King's House...' That stage of 10 miles took two and a half hours. Intense cold and rain meant that they arrived half-frozen. Their reception at the Kingshouse, once a byword for poor food and service, helped restore them: 'We got a fire directly, and in twenty minutes they served us up some kippered salmon, broiled; a broiled fowl; hot mutton ham and poached eggs; pancakes; oatcakes; wheaten bread; butter; bottled porter; hot water, lump sugar and whisky; of which we made a very hearty meal.' As elsewhere, once the railway line to Fort William was completed in 1895, the through coach became redundant. Some coachmen were reluctant to see that their day was over. Leslie Gardiner tells of one veteran

'The Old [Telford-age] and New [1930s] Roads'. As postcards like this suggest, the new 1930s roads were of great contemporary interest. (Author's collection)

The 'new' Glencoe road, with one of the few remaining milestones, was built in the early 1930s. It was welcomed by most, but traditionalists were appalled. (Author, 2019)

coachman who couldn't see the day when trains would get over Rannoch Moor the way the coaches did. Unfortunately for him, the trains did cross Rannoch Moor – and they still do.

All the way from Kingshouse to Bridge of Orchy, the next place of any significance, the scenery is truly spectacular, not least when passing Rannoch Moor, which some people find bleak and frightening but I find a place of drama and startling beauty. The name Bridge of Orchy derives from the original bridge constructed *c*. 1751 as part of Major Caulfeild's military road. The bridge we see now, though historic in its own right, is probably not the original and it is bypassed at any rate by the present-day road (see image on p. 87). The cottage across from the Bridge of Orchy Hotel bears the intriguing name of Stance Cottage. This derives from the fact that the ground here had been an overnight stance for cattle in droving days. The cattle, it is said, paid for the privilege of grazing at a stance in the form of their contribution to the fertility of the soil. An unusually green patch in a mainly brown moor may be an indication that this had once been a stance. Continuing south on the A82, the next stop is Tyndrum, which, especially since the West Highland Way was opened, has seen a considerable increase in the number of establishments catering for tourists. It is, of course, a junction, as this is where those bound for Oban, whether by road or rail, take their leave.

The highway between Fort William and Tyndrum built by Telford was a good one for its time. Any road, however, deteriorates without maintenance, and that was certainly the case with this one after the Government's Commission for Highland Roads and Bridges was wound up in 1862. County road boards and trusts took charge of the road network until 1889 when the newly created county councils took charge. The new councils, like their predecessors, tended to be dominated by the local landowners who, as a class, did not regard spending money on roads and bridges as a priority, and these suffered in consequence. Harry R. G. Inglis in his *Contour Road Book of Scotland* (1898) was highly critical of the road to the north of Tyndrum – a bad road, he wrote, with a very poor, stony surface as far as Inveroran. The rest of the road from Inveroran to Clachaig was even worse, with the Glencoe section, 'the cyclists Bete Noir,' generally in a very bad state. The trouble with the Tyndrum to Fort William road was that there had never been enough traffic in the past to justify the expense of improving it. Tourists going to the west and north from Glasgow found it easier to take a steamboat down the Clyde and then continue up the west coast to Oban and thence to Fort William. Once Oban and Fort William were connected by rail to Glasgow – Oban in 1880 and Fort William in 1895 – there was even less reason to invest in road building. Complaints about the state of the Ballachulish to Tyndrum road continued into the 1920s. For H. V. Morton, a bestselling author and journalist who toured the Highlands by car, it was the worst road in Scotland.

Kingshouse Inn on Rannoch Moor with Buachaille Etive Mor in the background. This is an 1881 image that was recycled in the 1930s by Valentine to sell as a postcard. (Author's collection)

Many people find Rannoch Moor dismal and bleak, but this image by my late son tells a different story. (Fraser Simpson, *c.* 2000)

As elsewhere in Scotland, it was the boom in motor transport in the interwar years that brought about a change in the government's policy. The increased number of motor vehicles brought demands for road widening and upgrading. In consequence, the national trunk road programme of road reconstruction, previously described, was extended to the road from Glasgow to Inverness via Glencoe and Fort William. Work on the road, which started just north of Tyndrum and rose to 1,143 feet at the summit, began in 1927, with the section to Fort William finished in 1933. The rest from Fort William to Inverness via the Great Glen was, as noted earlier, completed in 1934. The total length of the A82 now is 167 miles/269 km. The new highway, now classified as the A82, had its critics, with some people fearing the damage that would be caused to Glencoe in particular. Charles Plumb, who wrote dismissively of the changes wrought in Aviemore, was equally contemptuous of the new highway to Glencoe: 'of which enormity, as a walker, and even as a man, I cannot trust myself to speak with moderation.' Thomas Nichol, writing four years earlier in 1931 before the new road had been completed, hoped that the new road would be 'a pleasure in disguise to the wanderers with rucksack, for they will be left to tramp the old road unmolested, while their less fortunate brethren will be rushing through at top speed.' Unfortunately, as far as the grandest section, the Pass of Glencoe itself, was concerned, only disjointed sections of the old road were left for the wanderers to enjoy.

Inveroran Hotel in 1937 had been a drovers' inn with stance for cattle and sheep. It is now popular with anglers and hikers on the West Highland Way. (Author's collection)

Tinkers Changing Camp.

In the summer travellers like this family group were often to be met on Highland highways and byways. Usually they were welcomed, but sadly sometimes not. (Author's collection)

8

Tyndrum to Glasgow

Going south through Strath Fillan from Tyndrum, this section of the A82 is shared with the A85 as far as Crianlarich, and the A82 continues via Glen Falloch to Ardlui at the head of Loch Lomond and from there by the lochside road to Tarbet. In 1898 the *Contour Road Book* described the road down Loch Lomond to Balloch as 'especially good'. Black's 1910 *Guide* echoed this praise, but 'the plan most to be recommended' was to take the steamer from Balloch Pier and 'sail up through the beautiful archipelago that is the chief glory of Loch Lomond'. At that time, we are told, there were half a dozen points where one could take or leave the boat. For our Victorian tri-cyclist 'Nauticus' the ride along the loch was a delightful one. Today's road users will find the section from Ardlui to Tarbet more problematic. The delightful winding road, which the early tourists enthused over, presents problems for today's road users. From Tarbet to Balloch cyclists and pedestrians have the benefit of the mostly traffic-free West Lomond Cycle Path.

From the early days of tourism, when most tourists were travelling independently, Loch Lomond and Ben Lomond have been target destinations. In those days tourists like Dorothy and William Wordsworth and Samuel Taylor Coleridge were walking, riding on horseback or in some kind of carriage – in the case of the two Wordsworths it was an Irish jaunting car. The proprietors of humble inns that had catered mainly for cattle drovers found that they had to provide for well-to-do tourists. Judging by an 1852 guidebook they were now able to do this very well, with the inn at Tarbet being described as 'picturesque and comfortable' and that at Luss 'excellent'. In the early days of motoring, travel was no longer such a leisurely affair, nevertheless motorists were able to drive along by Loch Lomond and stop to enjoy the view. This was a time when motorists were able to enjoy the pleasure of weekend driving on roads that were comparatively traffic-free – 'the open road'. At the rush hours, at the beginning and end of the day, the joys of motoring could, however, rapidly dissipate.

For tourists coming from Glasgow and wishing to sail up the loch, Balloch at the foot of Loch Lomond was the obvious destination. Balloch was, and is, the principal departure point for boat tours of the loch. As a gateway to the Loch Lomond and Trossachs National Park, Balloch can offer the day visitor a choice of activities. One should be a visit to Balloch Pier where the historic paddle steamer *Maid of the Loch*

Loch Lomond at Ardlui.

This is the Loch Lomond road at a time when motorists were able to enjoy the pleasure of weekend driving on roads that were comparatively traffic-free: 'the open road'. (Author's collection)

THE CAMPING GROUND, LUSS, LOCH LOMOND AND BEN LOMOND

A more mobile population in the interwar years meant camp sites became popular, especially if they had a view, as here, of Ben Lomond. The old buses on this site would have been used as huts. (Author's collection)

is being renovated and hopefully eventually brought back into service. Balloch, just 20 miles from Glasgow, has long been a destination for Glaswegians seeking to enjoy loch and mountain scenery and to breathe in fresh air. In 1915 a far-sighted Glasgow Corporation purchased the Balloch Estate with its spacious parkland and castle and that ever since has been a magnet for visitors. The Balloch road is also for Glaswegians an escape route – at times a very crowded one. The road north from Balloch leads not just to Luss and other Loch Lomond tourist hotspots, but it is also the main highway to Oban, Fort William and Inverness. Once steamboat travel became accepted, tourists could sail from Balloch to Ardlui at the head of the loch and, for some years, even as far as Inverarnan via the canalised River Falloch, and thence by coach to the aforesaid towns.

From Balloch we are into the industrial belt with a choice of routes to Glasgow and the traveller here can make his or her own choice. 'Nauticus' in 1882, when leaving Glasgow, elected to go off to Loch Lomond by Dumbarton riding 'through a pleasant vale, with some pretty villas and pleasure grounds.' They – at this stage on the journey 'Nauticus' had a companion 'P' riding a bicycle – tried for an experiment a Temperance Hotel for their night's accommodation in Dumbarton. Their first temperance meal was not encouraging: 'wishy-washy tea, half-boiled eggs, a meagre allowance of bread and scrape, with a melancholy looking chap for a messmate.' In addition, 'Nauticus' had a problem with one of his tyres, a part of it coming loose. It was a solid tyre, of course; it would be some years yet before pneumatic tyres were on the market. To repair it he melted the loose part of the tyre with a candle and then bound the repaired section with string to hold it until the rubber hardened.

As cycling increased in popularity, the roads to and from Loch Lomond and other tourist destinations were once more in widespread use. At the end of the nineteenth century large numbers of cyclists like 'Nauticus' and his friend 'P' were wending their way into the Highlands via the Loch Lomond road. While 'Nauticus' departed from Glasgow by the Dumbarton road, this writer first approached the city by the same route via Dumbarton, but coming from the opposite direction. There were two of us and, having just left school in Buckie in north-east Scotland, we had embarked on a cycling tour of Scotland. That day in August 1948, we had cycled from Glen Nevis Youth Hostel and were bound for the not-long-opened Glasgow Hostel at No. 11, Woodlands Terrace. It was just three years after the war, and this was a very different Glasgow. There were not that many cars, but there were plenty of trams and tram lines which could bring you crashing down if you weren't careful. Since rationing was still in place, we carried temporary ration cards. My stay in Glasgow lasted longer than originally planned since my companion was summoned back to Buckie to play in a key football match – my friend incidentally later went on to play for Queen's Park and Glasgow Rangers. While he was away, I enjoyed a cultural feast, visiting art galleries and theatres including a George Bernard Shaw play at the Citizens. In the forties, experiences like that were in short supply in rural Banffshire.

The highways we cycled on in 1948 were basically little changed from pre-war days. The financial crisis of the early 1930s and then the Second World War meant that the kind of road reconstruction that had brought new roads to Glencoe and Loch Ness had come to an end. Some of the roads still in use then went far back in time. In many

Luss has long attracted visitors. It is now bypassed, but the loch provides direct access for those who arrive by boat. (Author, 2015)

A quiet day at Balloch. Some visitors would have been heading for the tearooms, others for the putting greens. (Author's collection)

Above: The *Prince Edward*, here at Balloch Pier, was a popular steamer on Loch Lomond from 1911 to 1955. Railway company coal trucks are on the pier ready to refuel her. (Author's collection)

Rigth: Visitors to Glasgow could explore the city and its environs by the city's extensive transport network using this 1934 *Corporation of Glasgow Transport Guide*. For trams now, though, you need to visit the city's excellent Transport Museum. (Author's collection)

parts of the Highlands, Thomas Telford would have found himself in familiar territory with quite a few of his bridges still in use. The roads might have been widened and tar-macadamised, and a few more passing places provided, but otherwise there was little difference. General Wade would also have been delighted to find his masterpiece, the bridge at Aberfeldy, still in everyday use. However, the need for traffic lights there would certainly puzzle him. What remains of the early motor age? Some of the roads and bridges of the twenties and thirties are of course still in use, maybe widened but otherwise little altered. There are other stretches of interwar roads now bypassed or left as laybys. Thanks to car enthusiasts we can also encounter restored examples of the vehicles of the interwar years.

As for the stagecoach era, little remains to remind us of what in this country was once a vibrant interlocking system of transport that, in its heyday, linked communities from Penzance in south-west England to the far north of Scotland. There are, nevertheless, some physical reminders of the stagecoach era in the form of former change inns – some genuine, others not – and old toll house. Milestones, it is sad to say, are fast disappearing – unnecessarily so in many cases. Some place names, however, survive to remind us of this period in our history. For example there is a Tollcross in both Glasgow and Edinburgh. In Fife there is the already referred-to Ferrytoll in Inverkeithing, and in Dunbartonshire the Allander Toll roundabout.

As for the benefits brought by the new ways to and through the glens, the last word should go to that great road and railway engineer Joseph Mitchell (1803–1883): 'The new roads in the Highlands acted like an irrigating stream in developing the productive powers of the country.'

Finishing with the joker in the pack, an Austin 7, snapped at Kingussie. More people were able to enjoy motor touring thanks to affordable cars like this wee two-tone Baby Austin. (Author, 2018)

Acknowledgments

I am indebted to many people who kindly gave assistance while I was writing this book. First and foremost are those who helped with proofreading: Anne Paterson, Rhona Mackenzie and George Robertson. Also Alan Brotchie, Professor David Munro and my late son Fraser Simpson for use of images and Dr Annie Tindley for pointing me to the Atholl Estate Office toll receipt thefts Extra thanks to George Robertson for his invaluable help in my quest for traces of the stagecoach era in Fife and Kinross. I am grateful too for the unstinting help given to me by the staff and volunteer helpers at many libraries, archive centres and heritage centres. The libraries include Dalgety Bay, Dunfermline, Edinburgh Central, Inverness, Kinross, Perth, Thurso and the National Library of Scotland. Perth and Inverness Archives were especially helpful, as were the volunteer helpers at the Brora and Helmsdale heritage centres and Fort William Museum. Nor should I omit the unknown photographers who, working for postcard firms like Raphael Tuck & Sons, J. B. White & Co. and J. Valentine & Sons Ltd, took many of the images I have reproduced here. Most of the images used in this book are either my own or from my personal collection. I must also express my thanks to the many authors whose works I have consulted. Only lack of space precludes me from listing them. My grateful thanks go to my editor Connor Stait and his colleagues at Amberley Publishing who have been working in difficult circumstance due to the outbreak in 2020 of the Covid-19 pandemic. Lastly, my apologies go to anyone whose name I have inadvertently omitted.

About the Author

Eric Simpson was historical adviser for the first four series of the popular BBC Scotland TV programmes *Grand Tours of Scotland*. He has written and lectured on many different aspects of Scottish history and heritage and is the author of many books and articles. His most recent Amberley titles are *Wish You Were Still Here: The Scottish Seaside Holiday* (2013) and *Hail Caledonia: The Lure of the Highlands and Islands* (2017). *Hail Caledonia and Highways* to the Highlands may be regarded as in many ways complementary works. The majority of the illustrations used in this book are the author's own either taken while travelling to and in the Highlands or from his archive collection. He is a native of Buckie, Banffshire, and now lives in Dalgety Bay, Fife.